From Your Daddy

Ann Franklin Bowes

ATHENA PRESS
LONDON

ISBN 1 84401 763 X

First Published 2006 by
ATHENA PRESS
Queen's House, 2 Holly Road
Twickenham TW1 4EG
United Kingdom

Printed for Athena Press

Dedicated

to the memory of Mary,

with love;

the finest mother any three girls could wish for.

Acknowledgements

Grateful thanks are due to the following, all of whom helped me in my quest, which took so long that many have sadly passed on:

Antigua and Barbuda High Commission in London; Barbara Ashton; Alfred and Joyce Clampitt; Den Clare; Neil Dalton; the late Elizabeth Glynis Davies; Elaine Delmar; the late Basil Drennan, Keble College, Oxford; Distinguished Emeritus Professor Clifton Orrin Dummett, University of Southern California; the late J Ingram Fox; Jeffrey P Green; Stephanie Hale, Ruskin College, Oxford; Dick Hannus; Hendon Register Office; Stephen Hogg; Brian Izzard; Ministry of Defence; Philip Moss, former Head Clerk of the University of Oxford; Peter D Manners, Church of Jesus Christ of Latter Day Saints Family History Library; Austin M Noltë; Oxford University Archives; Queen's College, Guyana; David Renwick, former editor of *Trinidad Express*; Howard Rye; Isla Smith, Keble College, Oxford; Cissie Thompson (née Izzard); Sheila Tracy, Radio 2; Ernest Weiler; the late Guilermo (Willie) Weiler; Stephen White; the late Alistair Wisker, Ruskin College, Oxford.

Very special thanks are due to Val Wilmer, without whom the above list of acknowledgements would have been considerably shorter.

I am grateful also to my husband, Herb, for his patient encouragement, and to my darling sons, Graham for urging me on, with enthusiasm, and Adam for running my errands in New York. Finally, to Elizabeth (Betty) McKitterick (née Franklin) for taking the time to read through my manuscript and, of course, to my dear sisters, Amba and Marjie.

One

I never had a daddy. I had a father, of course – how could I not? – but I never had a daddy. Or perhaps I should say that I had a daddy for a moment or two, because a moment or two is all the memory I have of him.

We are walking through the grounds of a large complex of council-owned flats in London on the way to visit my maternal grandmother. He is holding my little left hand. I examine his right one and observe with interest that the pale palm is a completely different colour from the back of his black hand. I haven't yet noticed that my own hands, although lighter in colour, have the same contrast between front and back. But I am only about eighteen months old.

Those moments are my only recollection of my father, although when he died I was thirty-four.

So far as my childhood and education are concerned, the notion of deprivation never occurred to me until I discovered how privileged my father's had been. From what I have learned, it would appear that he was brought up in a caring home with a professional father; he was taught music and became the organist of his church whilst still only fifteen; he went to the best public school in his country and won a scholarship to Oxford.

I think of my father as a sort of itinerant who casually wandered into my mother's life and then wandered out again, leaving two baby daughters by the way. As a child, my mother, Mary, had been deserted by her own mother, who ran off with a soldier. Twenty-five years later – or perhaps more than that – her mother approached Mary in Seven Sisters Road and identified herself and Mary, who was never a cruel or vicious woman, impulsively slapped her mother's face, the pain of the treachery returning instantly to her. She never forgave her mother. Yet it seems that Mum forgave my father the near-identical crime. She never spoke ill of him, always smiled when relating tales of her life with him. She would tell me that I looked like him and had his mannerisms, something I didn't want to hear. I didn't want to look like him or to be like him. I didn't want to be the colour he had made me; I wanted to have pink skin and light-coloured, straight hair like my mother. Mum had a daughter, Margery Hope, by a former marriage, whose father died in a road accident before the birth, and Marjie was very fair-skinned with blonde hair. I found the physical differences in our family very confusing.

Several years before her death, Mum moved into a pleasant, newly-built block of sheltered flats in Catford. Although she had lived all of her life north of the river in London, she decided to move nearer to Amba, my other sister, who lived on the outskirts of Kent. She was growing older and we all agreed that, in case of need, one of us ought to be able to get to her quickly. It was a courageous move on Mum's part, leaving behind the home she'd lived in and loved since just after the war and having to wave goodbye to her neighbours and her former life; but then she'd always been courageous and ready to take on whatever challenge presented itself and she settled happily in her new home. She made friends with her neighbours, a married couple, and when the wife died Mum and the widower, Albert, became good companions, sometimes taking holidays together.

I was there, in my mother's clean and bright new home, one day in 1974 and read the last letter my father had sent her. I'd had little, perhaps no, interest in my father ever. I regretted the fact that I had not had a father and I didn't hate him as Amba did, but I had no feelings for him except a fear that he would return, and that was a thought that terrified me. Yet I believed – hoped – that he wouldn't come back; he had become just a figment of imagination to me, almost an invented being, unreal, even though I was aware that in truth, of course, he really had existed. At that time I hadn't even seen a photograph of him and had no idea of what he looked like, although members of the family had described him as very handsome. No, I didn't want or expect him to come back into our lives, although I know that Mum always hoped he would. She had loved him and still loved his memory despite his desperately cruel treatment of her, and she continually told us how well-educated and talented he was, even mentioning him sometimes when his birthday came round.

How I came to see the letter I don't know; maybe I saw it by accident or Mum may have shown it to me. Whatever, that letter completely changed my feelings about my father; I was now interested in who he had been and wanted to know more about him and I hoped that what I might discover would please me. *I wanted to be pleased about my prodigal father!* I wasn't reading a passionate love letter, but his words displayed devotion and tenderness and it also expressed hopes for a happy and comfortable future with us all. It was, in parts, amusing and I could tell that my father had been not merely intelligent but also witty. So I was excited, surprised and impressed; but intrigued, too, because it struck me as impossible that a husband could write such a letter and then straight away desert his wife and children. Mum had told us about the tour to the West Indies and America with Zorina; there was never a time when we didn't know about it or about his disappearance, and it struck me as poignant – pitiful even – that Mum had preserved the letter for nearly forty years; it was now dog-eared and worn, yet she had kept it safe through all her difficulties and trials, throughout the war years and whenever she moved home, which had been many times, perhaps waiting for the day when it was right for us, his daughters, to read it. On one of the pages were pencilled scribbles where one of us, as a toddler, had presumably tried to make joined-up writing. I wanted to cry for my brave, dear mother.

Then and there I decided that I needed to know what had become of my father all those years ago, and to try to make some sense of his apparently callous behaviour. Mum said she wouldn't mind if I did some research on him, although she must have feared that she might be hurt yet again. She said I could keep the letter, and I placed it safely in a plastic envelope so that it wouldn't completely disintegrate.

Two

Sunday Evening Dec. 1st

My dear Mary,

*Today has been a quiet one for me. Last night I turned
in soon after dinner, about 9.40 I suppose, & before
long I was fast asleep; but before falling off I could feel
them weigh anchor & get going. The voyage is on the
rough side so far, & this morning I decided that the
horizontal position was best; so I stayed in bed, & had
some breakfast brought me there. At about 2.30 I had a
bath (salt-water), followed by a brisk shower (fresh-
water), & returned to bed. At first the Steward came
and cleared up a bit; & then I shaved, got my clavier
into position, did some other sorting-up, & got dressed.
It is now 6.45 & I am writing this before going into
dinner, which is at 7. Last night I enjoyed a fine dinner.
Tonight it will, I suppose, be just as fine – but the
question is whether I shall be able to enjoy it! I expect
the number of diners tonight will be far less than
yesterday; the purser says that by about Tuesday we
should strike the calmer part of the voyage.*

*I will try to write some short account of the journey
day by day; so by the time this reaches you it will be
quite a serial letter.*

It was in November 1935 that my father, Lushington Wendell Bruce-James, or Bruce Wendell as he was known for most of his life, breezed out of our lives when he set sail to begin what would be a concert tour of the West Indies and United States with a Russian opera singer called Zorina. Bruce was trying to establish a reputation as a concert pianist and he was to act as accompanist to Zorina on the tour. They were to meet their impresario, Hugo Larsen, when they arrived in the West Indies.

According to Amba's recollection, on the day he left the four of us waved our goodbyes from a tiny balcony with an iron railing that overlooked the street. We had moved from the house in Finchley, where I was born, into an upper flat in Grays Inn Road and apparently the four of us were all on that little balcony, waving down to Bruce as he climbed into the taxi that carried him away from us for ever.

During the sea crossing on the Dutch ship *Colombia*, Bruce wrote the long and loving letter to Mum, and after reading it and hearing how much Bruce looked forward to being reunited with his family, it must have been an almighty shock for Mum when she heard what Zorina and Larsen had to tell her. They returned to London some months later and invited her to dinner when they dropped the bombshell, although they did so with as much gentleness as was possible; Bruce, they told her, had decided to remain in the United States, and they weren't able to give an explanation. Mum later said that when she heard this she wanted to laugh in disbelief. Tragically, however, the information proved to be only too accurate. Bruce had left it to Zorina and Larsen to impart the news; a pretty despicable and cowardly act on his part. Perhaps he didn't even ask Zorina and Larsen to enlighten Mary; he might have been content to let her wait in vain, and it's even possible that his former companions had voluntarily taken on a compassionate role in putting her in the picture. We're talking here of an intelligent and cultured man, and the fact that he didn't contact Mary directly is something I find very hard to understand. I wish I could cry, Shame on you! but there can be no revenge; not even a slapped face. It's now apparent that he had no concern for his wife or for his infant children who must, to his eyes, have been standing in the way of his artistic progress. Were we all so very easy to forget? To abandon us all to poverty was unpardonable and, as Mum herself saw it, unbelievable and shocking. Of course, it might have been difficult for a couple in a mixed marriage to live in contentment in New York in the 1930s, I am aware of that; and Bruce had found it hard to pursue his dreams and career in England, but the self-serving solution he chose could be nothing but wrong – evil, even. The matter should surely have been discussed and suitable arrangements made – if there were such things as 'suitable arrangements'; simply to disappear was monstrous and desperately cruel, and as Bruce had been a man with religious beliefs, his behaviour must be regarded as a sin in the eyes of his God. Mary had married him in good faith and he had failed hideously in his obligations. I despise that selfish part of his character, and I hold my mother's memory in high regard, albeit with sorrow.

The music historian Howard Rye has been able to provide me with details of the tour. Zorina and Bruce gave concerts in December 1935 in Trinidad, then departed for Barbados and British Guiana; in January 1936 they performed in Surinam where they were afterwards entertained by the Governor on his private yacht; they then returned to Trinidad, and afterwards proceeded to Venezuela and Tobago.

In the *Barbados Advocate* of Monday, December 2 1935, Zorina is described as having 'the most powerful voice of any living soprano' and according to *The Daily Argosy*, of Friday, December 6 1935:

Madam Zorina, who is of Russian origin, has had a career as striking as her picturesque and commanding personality and includes triumphs in musical art, and heroic suffering and sacrifice during the Great War and the Russian revolution.

Born in Kiev of a noble Russian family, she embarked upon a dramatic career and when only sixteen years of age was given a role in comic opera. Within a year she married, and as the wife of an officer in the Imperial Army she could not appear on the public stage and so she studied medicine and music.

Then came the War, in which her husband was killed and on its conclusion, she returned to the concert platform.

The article features photographs of Hugo Larsen, Ekaterina Zorina and Bruce Wendell, with a brief history of each of them. Larsen is described as 'celebrated impresario', Zorina as 'world renowned prima donna', and Bruce Wendell as 'distinguished West Indies pianist'. It sounds like quite an impressive trio. Mr Bruce Wendell's story is very detailed; it mentions his father and his uncle, who 'still lives at St John's, Antigua'. It gives details of Bruce Wendell's childhood, through his university career to his war service in France. It tells how he studied in England and Budapest and had given recitals in leading concert halls in England; he is described as being a man of singular personal charm. But there, interestingly, his story ends, according to the newspaper. No mention is made anywhere of his marriage or of his children. The newspaper had been told nothing of us and it looks as though, in Bruce's consciousness, as soon as he left England we ceased to exist.

Yet another article appeared in *The Daily Chronicle*, Georgetown on Tuesday, January 7, 1936, this one entitled 'Oxford in My Time (by Bruce Wendell, in an interview)'. In it Bruce says, 'I went up to Keble because my mother wished me to go into the Church. Music was calling to me with notes ever more insistent. I do not believe that there was ever a time when, if I had been psycho-analyzed, it would not have been found that at the back of my mind was the intention to become a musician. But I did not feel a strong vocation to the Church, yet it was the wish of my people, and I decided to follow the course mapped out for me.'

The next part of the article is entitled 'Aristotle's Poetics Influenced Musical Life'. In it Bruce is quoted as saying, 'When [Aristotle] says of Tragedy that it must be "serious, entire, and of some magnitude" he writes ... of the great masterpieces of music. And unless the player is aware of the value of each of these words in a piece of music ... he cannot even attempt to interpret them...'

For me, that article is, I suppose, as important in trying to know Bruce Wendell as the letter to my mother. When I think of the difficult life she endured, I think that my mother's middle name should have been Tragedy. The triple tragedy of losing her mother, Marjie's father, and then Bruce.

The tragedy Bruce presented to my mother was all of the things he mentions in his *Daily Chronicle* interview. It was serious; it was entire; it was of some magnitude. She was undoubtedly aware of the value of each of those words in her life. What's more, she did interpret them successfully and eventually overcame her problems. My father's tragedy, on the other hand, was that despite tossing aside his wife and children, his ambitions were never fulfilled. He states that 'through pity and terror [Tragedy] corrects and refines the passions'. I hope he pondered that philosophy in later life.

During the First World War Bruce was posted to France with the University Corps, Royal Fusiliers. In the same article, above, he says, 'I joined the 12th and later the 19th Battalion, Royal Fusiliers (Public School Corps), and there music pursued me still. I was appointed organist of the battalion, and with certain chosen friends, who represented the choir, used to dodge parades, going off solemnly to almost entirely mythical choir practices.' Of that time I was told a story which may or may not be apocryphal: Bruce joined the Officers' Training Corps at Oxford, but when a prominent member of the Royal Family – possibly His Majesty himself – came to review the troop he said, indicating Bruce, 'Who is he? There are no black officers in the Army,' and he refused to review the men until Bruce was sent off. In the Keble College list in the *University Roll of Service (1920)*, his entry reads: '1910 Bruce-James, L.W. Pte. R. Fusiliers. (Discharged.)' so the incident may be true. I contacted the Ministry of Defence for information about him from service records, but unfortunately none could be traced relating to Bruce's military service in the 1914–18 war as a large proportion of the records of soldiers who served during that period were totally destroyed by enemy air action in 1940. It would seem, I was told, that Bruce's records were among them.

Three

Monday Evening Dec. 2nd

Last night was a blower, & no doubt about it. After an excellent dinner, followed by coffee in the social room – where the orchestra played (violin, cello, & piano) – I went off early to bed. I soon got off to sleep, having locked myself into my cabin, but before dozing off was conscious that the ship was rolling a bit; however during the night I woke up to find that we were in the midst of a gale all right, & I could hear from the snippets of conversation that some neighbour of mine had to turn out, owing to his port-holes being stove in by an enormous wave. Luckily for him the pieces of glass did not actually hit him. All this I learned later today, as I refused to budge at the time & finally went off to sleep again. Today I decided to appear for lunch, & found myself thoroughly enjoying a huge meal. After that I retired to rest again, reading in my cabin until 6.15 when I bathed and dressed & now I shall be going into dinner.

I was ashamed and embarrassed about my father having 'gone away and not come back' for most of my young life – even until I was married with children of my own – and I wished I could have referred to 'my parents' instead of 'my mother'

17

like most of my friends. It was bad enough looking different from everyone else; having an 'incomplete' family made matters worse. I hesitated even to tell my sons about my father's desertion when they were old enough to understand and I certainly wouldn't have volunteered the information to mere acquaintances; maybe a close friend or two, but then only if questioned about him. The shame and embarrassment I felt was compounded by the fact that my father was black, although I don't really understand why *I* felt such dishonour about his clearing off. My colour was, however, something that made me feel permanently self-conscious. Rarely, very rarely indeed, did I ever see another black person and when that happened I was unsure of how to behave. Should I smile at them or should I ignore them as I would if I met a stranger who was white? It was so puzzling. When I was seven or eight and evacuated to the country during the war, there was a game I played with friends when walking back from school together; we had to be sure not to tread on the cracks between the paving stones otherwise we would marry a black man; a dire warning that troubled me more than a little. (This game may have originated from the fact that 'black man' was the term traditionally used in folklore to describe a hobgoblin or bogeyman or other imaginary monster and that it was such a creature we would marry if we trod on the cracks.) The strange thing was that none of my friends thought it odd that I should join in the game; they didn't seem to notice that I was black, or think that I might be offended. Perhaps they thought that even I, being the colour I was, shouldn't marry a black man because that seemed to be the worst thing that could possibly occur. Look what had happened to Mummy! But my friends couldn't have understood the game either and probably none of them had ever seen another black person, except maybe in books or movies. Nonetheless, I thought that I would never be married, because no white man would want me and I couldn't marry a black man. I always felt uncomfortable about joining in the game; the feared upshot of stepping on the cracks was something I couldn't get my head around. I was torn between being black yet feeling and acting white; Amba and I had no one to consult about this dilemma because we knew no black grown-ups. So I continued to pretend to be white, and the pretence seemed to succeed with everyone who knew me. My colour was only brought to my attention by strangers who stared at me (how I hated it!), sometimes admiringly or in some cases whilst calling out names such as 'blackie' or 'nigger'. I learned to ignore such jibes, which were just a form of bullying, after all; but there was one occasion when I was very offended.

It happened when Miss Watkinson, our form mistress who was also our French teacher, took the class one day on a trip to Hampton Court Palace. There was a group of French people near us in the palace courtyard and one of the party, a woman, said to a companion, *'Quelle joli petite négresse!'* I had seen her looking and smiling at me and, because I was trying to avoid the attention as usual, didn't hear exactly what she said.

Miss Watkinson waited until we were out of earshot of the French party, then asked me, 'Did you understand what that French woman said, Ann?'

'I'm not sure,' I replied.

Miss Watkinson repeated the comment in French and, with a smile, translated it: 'What a pretty little negress!'

I was outraged! Pretty little negress, indeed! What a patronising and arrogant French woman! What about pretty little *girl*? I was about thirteen at the time and it was a ridiculous reaction on my part; or it would be a ridiculous reaction today. 'Then', however, was a very different country. I didn't let Miss Watkinson realise that I was wounded by the remark; but I was.

Our exotic appearance often prompted questions about our father, which I dreaded and hated, and so I would invent stories rather than tell the truth. Sometimes I would pretend he was a missionary on service overseas, an explanation that I thought sounded rather romantic (Mum had said that he had, at an earlier age, considered going into the church ministry, a fact later confirmed in the newspaper interview). On other occasions I would say that he was fighting abroad, or had been dead since I was small. It wasn't until I was about sixteen that I forced myself to overcome this habit of lying about my father; after all, I wasn't to blame for his desertion. So then I would either not respond to the questions or, reluctantly, reveal the truth with as much equanimity as I could conjure up, as though it had never bothered me. Mummy, however, persisted in trying to tell us about our father. Wigmore Hall in London first became known to me because she told me he had performed there; and then there were the stories of the other entertainers he brought home; of the adventure when, whilst she'd been pregnant, he'd taken her across London to buy an Armstrong Siddeley motor car, had listened to a few cursory instructions from the salesman and then had brought them both home in the luxurious limousine although he had never driven before. It was a wonder to her, she said, that they survived the journey! What she was trying to do, I think, was to 'educate' us about our father, in case he should return. *For when he would return.* I'm sure she hoped for this for most, if not all, of her life. Poor Mummy! To yearn for the man she had loved to come back to her yet to know, at the same time, that his daughters would never welcome him must have been very saddening. Neither Amba nor I wanted to hear about him; never wanted to know anything about the man who had deserted us and had left us feeling like little black oddities in a white world. I hoped he would never return; it was – always – too late for me to welcome back my father.

The Jamaica Times of September 19, 1936, described Bruce as a 'man with a university education ... an enviable war record and a decided journalistic flair [who] says frankly that he turned to music as a means of livelihood, not merely as a pastime, because in a white country (England) racial prejudice barred the door to a military profession or to a staff job in the writing game'. I don't think I'm being unreasonable in thinking that that statement is loaded with hypocrisy. Even bearing in mind, as I do, the humiliation Bruce had allegedly suffered whilst in the Officers' Training Corps at Oxford, to say that to live in England in the 1930s with its prevailing racial prejudice meant that black people were unable to pursue their chosen professions does seem like a backhand slap in the face for the two black daughters he abandoned to face the racist music alone. Further, he had so far done nothing, and would always do nothing, to help those daughters receive an education that might give *them* the opportunity of choosing a profession. That task he irresponsibly left to our mother, and after passing our eleven-plus exams we were sent to a fine little school where we were prepared for decent employment. Had our father been around to guide us we might also have gone into higher education, but as things stood financially, that was totally out of the question.

I wouldn't mind betting that Bruce's family knew nothing of his marriage to our mother or of his children. He was born on the island of Antigua on 9 February 1891. His father, Thomas Bruce-James, is described on Bruce's birth certificate as a teacher at Music Institution City. Most of the family were educationists, and his uncle, Joseph James, who was a Schools Inspector, was awarded the MBE in the 1930 New Year Honours. The entry in *The Times* dated Wednesday, January 1 1930 reads: 'James, Joseph Edward, Esq., Local Inspector of Schools, Presidency of Saint Christopher and Nevis' (St Christopher is now more commonly known as St Kitts). It is clear, therefore, that Bruce came from an educated and influential family. They moved to Guyana (then British Guiana) whilst Bruce was a child and, from age six to eleven he attended Mr Sharples' Schools, a primary school where he was a classmate of Eglantine Annabella Dummett (née Johnson) who was born in 1892. I learned about this during a telephone conversation with Professor Clifton Orrin Dummett, Eglantine's son. She later became the aunt of the jazz musician Ken 'Snakehips' Johnson, who was killed in an air raid in London when the Café de Paris, where he was performing, received a direct hit in March 1941.

In contrast, my mother, Mary Clampitt, was of humble origin. She was born on 8 September 1905 in St Pancras, London, England, the daughter of a timber merchant's assistant. Theirs was a working-class family and when Mary and her younger brother, Bill, were still children, their mother deserted the family for 'a soldier in a red jacket', a traumatic event that had a great influence on Mary; throughout her life she was unfailingly loyal to those who loved her and whom she loved. Mary's father later took a second wife, whom my sisters and I thought of as our grandmother, and three more children were born: John, Emily and Alfred.

Mary Clampitt and Bruce Wendell came from different worlds, geographically, culturally and academically. Mary's impoverished family had to struggle to make ends meet, and as soon as Mary was employed she helped her parents financially. Her father died whilst only in his fifties; there was no spare cash for luxuries and only just enough for the essentials of living, and an education for any one of the family that might come near to matching Bruce Wendell's was unthinkable. In her various places of employment, Mary observed others in higher positions and although she never put on airs and graces, she learned how to behave in polite society. She taught us how to set a table, how to serve a meal in the correct way and she also described to us how we would be expected to behave if invited to smart functions. And as the world became more sophisticated her manners never disgraced herself or us.

'Did he have false teeth?' I asked, the first time I saw a photograph of my father.

'Of course not,' retorted Mum, but she smiled, pleased that I wanted to know something about him.

I thought what a classically handsome face he had, and the white teeth sparkling out from a broad smile were dental perfection.

Mary always had a happy face, despite the hard life she led; her beautiful, heavy-lidded eyes were the brightest, most twinkling cornflower blue, set deeply in an attractive, hollow-cheeked face which, like several members of the Clampitt family, featured a narrow and slightly pointed nose; she had a smile always at the ready, and when we were children she wore her shoulder-length brown hair parted simply on one side, held in a clip and rolled up at the bottom, as was the fashion. She wore very little make-up and the smell of her possessions – perhaps a purse or a scarf or some other small item – when I was little and during the years of our separation was to me a comforting mixture of face powder, tobacco and leather; I loved that smell and would bury my nose in one of her scarves or gloves. I would have been able to tell from the scent of any of the things she wore that they belonged to my mother.

As I write this account, only Uncle Alfred, the youngest, survives from that generation, and he and his wife, Joyce, have helped me to piece together much of this story. When I first started writing it I had a long telephone conversation with Alfred; he, too, was interested in knowing what had become of Bruce, and he encouraged my research. He told me that shortly before he left England, Bruce had applied to the BBC for the job of resident organist, a position he had high hopes of getting, but the successful applicant had been Reginald Foort, who held the post for many years. This I had also learned from Mum. I remembered Reginald Foort; he was a white man, and the family thought that Bruce had been passed over because of his colour.

Alfred said that it was not Bruce's intention to leave us. What he was trying to achieve was a better life for us all. He told me that Bruce was a gentleman.

In that case, I wanted to know, why hadn't Bruce been in touch with us with some sort of explanation. *Ever?*

That question Alfred couldn't answer; yet he was adamant that Bruce had loved my mother and had not intended, at the outset, to leave for good.

It had been, without doubt, a difficult time in Britain for ambitious black people, and Alfred reiterated that it was because of this that Bruce decided to embark on the concert tour. Alfred remains very loyal to the memory of Bruce Wendell. I was not convinced.

Mary was an intelligent girl who had received a basic education and later did various jobs: some domestic work; a Lyons Corner House 'nippy' (waitress); shop assistant in the West End department store Debenham and Freebody; cinema usherette. She was a hard worker and always remained so, then, and in the later, harder years. Alfred told me that, had it not been for Mary, his family would not have known what Christmas was; Mary gave her family Christmas, and Alfred talks lovingly of his sister. She provided food and presents for her siblings at Christmas – even, one year, a bicycle for John, who was instructed to share it with his younger brother. When he was old enough Bill went to Kneller Hall, trained as a bandsman and served in the army and later, after World War Two, worked for the War Department until retirement. Bill didn't keep in touch with any of his family except us; there was some sort of estrangement between them but I never really knew what that was. We saw a lot of him and of his wife Doris and their family.

Four

Tuesday afternoon 3.45 p.m.

Today I am writing rather earlier. I was up for breakfast at 8 o'clock this morning, & enjoyed the meal thoroughly. Sat & read on deck after that until lunch-time, when I felt that to have lunch would about make me bust. Why I finished breakfast I suppose round about 9, & at 11.15 the deck-steward handed out beef-tea & a biscuit, then fancy asking one to lunch at 12.30. And what a breakfast! Grape Fruit, Omelette with Bacon, Brown Bread & Butter galore, 2 Buns with Butter ad lib., Marmalade, Coffee.

So it was that some time during 1931 Bruce and Mary met whilst both were employed at the RKO Theatre (known originally as The Leicester Square Theatre), she as an usherette and he as the cinema organist, and they married at Hampstead Register Office in 1932. At that time both their fathers were dead, Bruce's (now described on the marriage certificate as Agricultural Instructor) having died before Bruce went up to Oxford. Shortly after they married, my sister, Amba, was born and the following year I arrived. Amba's full name is Amba Mary Bruce Amanda, the initials of each separate name spelling the first with both parents' names embedded in the centre. I was named Anne Viola Luleta, although somewhere along the way I have carelessly discarded or lost the 'e' at the end of Anne.

The family lived in Broadhurst Gardens, Hampstead, and later in North Crescent, Finchley, where I was born. Amba and Marjie both have some memory of Bruce. Marjie tells how she used to sit with him at the baby grand piano in the drawing room, and how the bedrooms in North Crescent had names: the Lemon Room; the Pink Room; the Blue Room, which was our parents'. Amba remembers trying to prise open one of Bruce's eyes when she came across him asleep on a sofa one day. I recall nothing very clearly of the period although there was a small dog named Trixie whom I vaguely remember, and a doll's pram I caught my hand in when tightening up its hood; I still have a scar on my right palm and what comes to mind is a copious amount of blood and a lot of howling. Mum loved that house; she sometimes described it to us and one of her prized possessions was the Ideal boiler that provided hot water; she had never been used to such personal luxury. She was at first aware of a certain hostility from those living nearby because of Bruce's colour, but she told me how one day he had been practising at the piano and, unexpectedly, had received applause from some of the neighbours who were outside and who had been listening to the music; the ice had been broken.

In the 1930s the 'coloured' (as they were then known) show business people in London all seemed to know one another. Alfred told me that Mum wouldn't always take Bruce into her family's home when she visited them so Bruce would park his car a little way away, down by the coal bays where the poor local people would collect bits of fuel. Alfred liked and admired Bruce and Bruce seemed to be fond of his young brother-in-law, aged about twelve at the time, so they would sit in the car and talk together whilst Mary was indoors. Alfred told me, 'One day, when I was a child, Bruce came in the car to collect Granny and me. This was a great thrill for me, to be taken out in a car, perhaps with some of my friends looking on. Bruce said he was going to give us a surprise, and took us to your house. When we arrived there, the entertainer Leslie "Hutch" Hutchinson was in the house sitting at the piano waiting to perform for us.' He added, 'That was the way Bruce was. We were just poor people, but he included us in activities as though we were of the same class as himself.'

Mary, when she got the opportunity of making us listen, told us how she had met 'Hutch' and the singer Elisabeth Welch and that Amba, as an infant, had been cradled by Paul Robeson who had sung her a lullaby. She had enjoyed her life with our father and was always ready to talk about it. She had been content; she had had a fine home, a loving and talented husband and three healthy daughters with what looked like assured futures, and she had also seemed better placed to help her family. We had all been happy.

'Mary lived the life of a lady then,' Alfred explained, 'which made the next chapters of her life doubly hard.'

What Mary never talked about, though, was Marjie's father, and he remains a mysterious shadow in our background. Until I began to piece together this tale I had always been under the impression that when Mum was pregnant and her husband was killed in a motorcycle accident it had been revealed that he had married her bigamously. Marjie pleaded to know about him, to know who he had been, but for reasons steadfastly unexplained, Mum would never, ever discuss him. She was adamant; no comment. It was clear that she had somehow been wounded so deeply as far as Marjie's father was concerned that she couldn't bear to confront her scars. I expect Uncle Bill would have been able to shed some light but he was dead by the time I took an interest. All we know is that Marjie's father's name was Hughes (no first name), that he was blond and that he and his brother had some sort of hairdressing business. We always knew that his death occurred before Marjie was born, but it was a great shock to my sister to see on her birth certificate that her father is described as 'Unknown'. I tried, without success, to find the marriage certificate of Mary and Hughes; although Hughes is a fairly common name, I had expected Mary's maiden name of Clampitt to produce some results, but I found nothing and later discovered that in those days (1928) if a child was born posthumously outside of marriage 'Unknown' was the required definition of the dead father. Yet on Bruce and Mary's marriage certificate she is described as Mary Hughes, aged 26, 'Widow'. Something doesn't add up, so I asked Alfred about this mystery and he believes that Mary and the man Hughes were not married; that Hughes was already married to another but that they had hoped to marry in the future. Whatever the truth of the matter it must have been a seriously agonising situation; Mum's resolve not to explain didn't once waiver and she took her secret to the grave, never satisfying Marjie's curiosity about a father she really did have a right to know about. One tiny clue is that our mother was a deeply superstitious woman who was very, very suspicious of blond-haired men, so that when I met my first husband who had the same colouring she was very sceptical about our relationship, although she soon discovered that he was a man to be trusted. Maybe she had been deceived by Hughes; if so, Mum had more than her share of bad luck as far as men were concerned.

Because I was so young and have little memory of the pre-war years, I have had to rely heavily on what I have been told or have discovered later about that time. When I made the acquaintance of Val Wilmer, the jazz journalist, a great deal was revealed. This story could not have been completed without Val's help. It is a strange and sad thing to say about my own father, but I have learned more about him since meeting Val than in all the years before. The writers Jeffrey Green and Howard Rye, to whom Val referred me, and Val herself, have known Bruce Wendell more closely through their separate careers than I, his daughter, have. When I first started to seek explanations for his defection I would have been eager to read more about him had I known that others had mentioned him in their own works.

Val also introduced me to Den Clare, the son of 1930s string bassist Abe 'Pops' Clare, who told me when I went to see him at his home that Bruce used to visit the Clare family when Den was about fourteen and that he often spoke of his own young family.

'What sort of voice did he have?' I wanted to know.

'Oh,' he replied, 'a light West Indian lilt.' I tried to imagine it and I was sorry, but only for myself, that Den had memories of my father while I had almost none.

Both 'Pops' Clare and Bruce Wendell played cinema organ for silent films. Val Wilmer sent me a copy of a two-page article by Bruce published in *The Melody Maker (Music in the Kinema)* of September 1928. At that time he was calling himself Wendell Bruce-James (he seemed to take quite a while to settle on a name he would find most comfortable; there appear to be several different aliases). The article was entitled 'The Ideal Kinema Organ'. I don't know enough about music to be able to critically analyse the article competently, but it seems to be an interesting and, I think, skilful description of the basic essentials of the instrumental accompaniment to what Bruce called the 'Silent Drama'. The introduction giving details about the author states that Bruce had been engaged earlier at the Grange Kinema, Kilburn, the Coronet Theatre, Notting Hill Gate, the Globe Kinema, Acton and the Angel, Islington, so it would appear that he was a proficient cinema organist.

I was taken aback by how much material had been published by or about Bruce Wendell. Val pointed me in the direction of several newspaper articles, one of which was in the Music column of *The Jamaica Times* of 19 September, 1936. It was entitled 'How Important is Jazz? discussed by Bruce Wendell', and includes the following passage:

> Hearing him perform at one of the big concert halls in London, it is with no small surprise, shock almost, that one goes into a picture house and as the curtains part, the letters, W E N D E L L, flash, huge and glaring, on the screen. Then a huge jazz organ rises slowly into view and before it, half-turned towards the audience and with his fingers poised on the keyboard, sits Wendell. The English audience settles back comfortably. The Guianese knows his business, they wait for his music with that same happy expectation that a very different type of audience awaits the very different type of music of which Wendell is equally capable of making.

(Bruce was sometimes described as Guianese because of the length of time he had lived in British Guiana.)

Den Clare also told me that his parents were very troubled when they heard that Bruce had decided to go to the United States; and he echoed Alfred's words: 'Bruce was a gentleman'. Den explained that Bruce was very kind to him as a child, and had given him violin lessons. One day he allowed Den to ride up onto the stage on the organ seat between performances (at the Super Cinema, Gravesend), and Den was the envy of his classmates when they heard about his experience. Den is also a musician, and before I left him, he played me a few pieces on his guitar.

Den's family didn't hear from Bruce after he left England, but from what Den has told me about his family, I wouldn't be surprised if, had they known that Mary had been deserted, they would have provided her with some moral support.

Amba and her husband once took Mum to see the performer Nat King Cole at the London Palladium. As he sang the song *Unforgettable*, tears streamed from Mum's eyes.

That must have been more than twenty years since she'd last seen Bruce. How could he have deserted her without so much as an explanation? Even a feeble excuse would have been better that nothing; he acted in a despicable, spineless way. He took from us his love, if there was any, his intellect, his talent, his culture and, of course, his physical presence as a father and protector. I'm sure, too, that my own lack of self-confidence and self-esteem was due to his disappearance. He would have been well aware that he'd left our mother a huge burden. She had to care for our emotional, spiritual and material needs, something she did well at a time when there was no Welfare State to assist her or, indeed, family members who would or were able to help. Bruce must have loved her at some time (she told me that he'd pursued her for six months before they became close) and maybe he judged that somehow she'd survive it all despite the fact that her circumstances were worsened because two of her fatherless daughters were black. Still, at the time I wanted no part of Bruce Wendell; I merely accepted our mother's sacrifices with a child's selfishness.

When I told her I'd try to find out what had happened to Bruce, I'm sure Mum hoped that I would trace him, and I wondered whether she had ever attempted the task herself. The world was a bigger place in the pre-war years, of course; it would have cost a great deal of money for her to have taken on such a search. It took me ages to find him – mainly because I lost interest for long periods and had days of idleness and tedium that alternated with those of great enthusiasm. I had the help of quite a lot of people eventually, and although I didn't know it at the time, Bruce Wendell was already dead at the start of my enquiries.

I shared Amba's feelings about not wanting our father to return to the family and yet, as a child, I also wanted, deep down inside, to have a special dad like most of my friends and all the children in the books I read. If only, I thought, everything could end happily and I could be transformed into an 'ordinary' child in an 'ordinary' family; if only I were not so 'noticeable'. I seemed always to be evading the stares of strangers and I was adept at avoiding eye contact with the curious whilst always being aware of their interest. Of course, it would have been so much easier had Bruce died; at least that would have been honourable and then I might have been able to idealise my lies about him. All the stories our mother had told us about our father, though – or tried to tell us – had seemed fanciful and I regret to say that, at the time, I just didn't believe some of them. It all seemed to me too fantastic. We were not connected with talented and intellectual people and it was impossible for me to accept that at one time we had been.

Later, everything Mum told us proved to be true.

Five

So instead of going in to lunch I had an orange & a
pear on deck. I then went over to the Second Class to
see Dr James, & spent an hour chatting with him. He is
the same as ever, inclined a bit to brood on unpleasant,
rather than enjoy & make the most of, the pleasant
occurrences in life. So back to some more reading.
From 4 o'clock till 5 tea is available, & after a cup I
shall retire, until my bath at 6.15.

In April 1937 Bruce gave a recital at the Town Hall on West 43rd Street, New York.

After the shock of realising what a desperate predicament she was now in, Mummy assessed her options and put the furniture into storage (which later, during the war, was bombed and destroyed) and we moved into rooms on the first floor of a house in Ireton Road, Upper Holloway, fairly close to our grandmother. It was a dreary place, that's about the best I can say of it; the house was on three storeys and was shared by several families, as was the solitary lavatory, and there was no bathroom or even a proper kitchen. A stove stood on the landing, where Mum cooked our meals, but because the stairway was a communal one anyone could see what was being prepared and, according to Uncle Alfred, one of the tenants, a woman who was known as Old Soap, thought nothing of stealing dumplings out of our stews. Old Soap was a very dirty and scruffy person who sometimes gave us a penny or halfpenny to buy some sweets, but Amba tells me that we were never sure whether to accept because we didn't know how close the coin may have been to her filthy body! It must have been a dreadful come-down for Mum, although she put her pride in her pocket and accepted the circumstances.

One of the families in the house was named Peach, and my sisters and I devised a splendid game whenever we had tinned peaches for tea. One of us would say, 'I'm eating David Peach.'

Then another of us would pick up a piece of peach on her spoon, saying, 'This is Mr Peach,' before popping the fruit into her mouth.

Then the third would join in: 'And here goes Mrs Peach. Yum, yum.' And we would all shriek with laughter; how hilarious it was! Oh, it was a wonderful game.

'Shh!' Mummy admonished. 'Supposing they should hear you!'

But it was far too entertaining and we continued to play our game whenever we had tinned peaches. Anyway, we were sure the Peaches wouldn't mind; they'd probably heard it all before.

Another tenant was a man who seemed at the time to be incredibly ancient; I think his name was Mr Webster. He lived immediately above us and regularly sat at his front window chewing tobacco. Every now and then he spat huge quantities of dark brown saliva on to the window sill and sometimes it would drip down on to ours. I was once in his room for some reason, and found the dreadful stains on his window sill horribly fascinating.

I had already learned to read by the time I was five, and whilst we were living in Ireton Road I had a large, hard-backed reading book full of children's stories called *Let's*

Pretend,[1] and the front cover was illustrated with a smiling boy and girl dressed in grown-up clothes that were, of course, much too large; the girl wore high-heeled shoes which extended back past her ankles. I read that book, with Mummy's help, from the first to last page. The back cover featured an advertisement for condensed milk,[2] and I read it so many times I knew it off by heart. As far as I was aware I'd never been to a birthday party or had one of my own. This advertisement pictured a table spread with party fare and surrounded by happy children, and the advertisement went:

'Bread and milk at a party? But the curious thing was that the children liked it better than the cakes.'

Condensed milk – how we loved it! We often scoffed slices of bread spread with condensed milk; Mummy was aware of the need for healthy eating, so we had plenty of fruit, too, such as banana sandwiches or banana custard and I liked tangerines because I could peel them. I found it impossible to get the peel off an orange, so when there were no tangerines I took my orange to Marjie. 'Peel my orange, Marj,' I'd plead. She tells me that she tired of this repeated request, but always helped me.

Children's games, back then, were seasonal. At a certain time of the year every boy and girl would somehow simultaneously acquire a whip and top, or obtain an empty can with which to play 'Tin Can Tommy', a chasing game. Then at some other time, everyone would be skipping with ropes or playing 'stones', a game of skill which required seeing how many stones you could pick up with one hand whilst tossing another into the air and catching it again with the same hand.

---

[1] I have been unable to trace the copyright holder of this volume, despite making every effort.

[2] The advertisement was for Nestlés condensed milk; I contacted Nestlé who were unable to identify the advertisement and they gave me permission to use the quotation.

Unlike children's toys and games of today, those of our childhood were inexpensive and, sometimes, home-made; boys constructed their own scooters from planks of wood and ball-bearing wheels, and a boy riding a manufactured, bought scooter would be considered as either a real cissie or very posh. Mummy always made sure that we were in the 'game fashion' of the time.

I got into real trouble the day we all had small, framed slates and a packet of coloured chalks. I was sitting on the front step of the house busily working with my slate and chalks, but after a time I tired of this and placed the slate, with the chalks, just inside the open front door and went off in pursuit of some other activity. I had been very careful not to break any of my chalks. When I returned, the slate and chalks were missing. I looked around and saw a small boy a few doors down busily drawing on a slate which rested on his lap, and I was angry to see that some of the chalks he was using were broken. I snatched both chalks and slate away from the boy, gave him a slight punch, and triumphantly returned to my front door, where I sat down and continued with my art. A short time later the small boy's mother, dragging her howling son behind her, came up to me and demanded that I return his possessions but I refused, saying they were mine. Mummy came downstairs to see what was going on and to my surprise said that she'd taken my slate and chalks upstairs for safety. Then she felt obliged to apologise to the boy and his mother for my behaviour; that taught me not to jump to the wrong conclusion. Mummy scolded me and I was sorry, but at least I'd had the self-confidence then to insist on having returned to me something that I thought was my own, even accompanying the demand with minor violence. Throughout the rest of my childhood that confidence evaporated completely; I would allow anyone to say or do what they liked at my expense and I never stuck up for myself again. On one occasion, at secondary school, I noticed that another girl at school was using a very distinctive fountain pen – it looked like mother-of-pearl – which I had earlier owned and lost, but I didn't have the courage to ask the girl to give it back to me; I told Amba, and Amba sorted it out. My assertiveness was very soon to leave me after the slate and chalks incident.

Mummy usually took on at least two jobs at a time; she was determined to support us and to keep us all together. How on earth she managed, I can't imagine. Sometimes she took us with her to one of her cleaning jobs; I have a faint recollection of us having great fun sliding down a laundry chute and landing on a pile of linen in a shop where she worked. After making sure we were safely asleep in the evenings she went shopping for food; some of the stores stayed open late at night. In those pre-war days she endured such personal privation that her health suffered; she was extremely thin (although she plumped out a bit in middle age when most of her troubles were behind her); she developed a stomach ulcer which never fully healed all her life and required hospital treatment on more than one occasion; and, from time to time and over many years, she suffered from alopecia, a worrying hair loss that left bald patches on her head (I nearly described this as a *distressing* hair loss, but that sounds like a pun and it was certainly no joke).

We children sometimes spent a few days with Aunty Kitty who lived at Church End, Finchley. We called her 'Aunty' although she was not actually a relative but Amba's godmother and the only one of Bruce's acquaintances in London who gave Mum any sort of support. She had no children of her own and was the widow of a black GP; she and her late husband had been long-standing friends of Bruce. Aunty Kitty lived in a large, old house; there was heavy mahogany furniture and 'magic' drawing books. We loved to visit her and her mother, who was Granny Robson to us, and by looking after us for a few days she allowed Mummy some respite from her difficult life. After the war white-haired, slender Granny Robson remarried at the age of eighty, and we were all invited to her wedding.

We were by this time living in real poverty, riches to rags – although I realise now that Bruce was not actually rich, it was just that he liked to live stylishly; it may have been what he had become used to. I had, as a baby, developed pneumonia (apparently I had received violet ray treatment for this illness, which must have been the reason, I explained to myself when I noticed that I was different from everyone else, that my skin was tanned!) and I had been cared for by a nanny. She must have been a kind-hearted woman and she kept in touch with Mummy so that when she heard that Bruce had deserted his family she offered to take care of me, even suggesting adoption. Mummy's eldest brother, Bill, and his wife, Doris, on the other hand, announced that Mummy's predicament was of her own making.

'She should never have married a black man,' Aunt Doris announced.

'Unless she puts the girls into an orphanage, her life is ruined,' Uncle Bill declared.

He actually repeated this avuncular opinion to Amba many years later whilst he was a guest at her home. Although Mummy and Bill always remained very close, Aunt Doris refused to speak to Mummy for years, obviously considering Mary's behaviour too shameful. Did she believe that Mary was the black sheep of the family? Or maybe a scarlet woman? Mary was neither of those things; if a black sheep of the family existed it had to be Bruce, and as for being a scarlet woman, well – Mary turned out to be more like a saint. Naturally she would have been the subject of gossip; not only did she have a yellow-haired, fatherless child, she also had two little black fatherless children – a scandalous situation in those days so that she may well have appeared, to some, to be a scarlet woman. Whatever, Aunt Doris had much too generous a nature to persist in her silence; she later came round and became a kind and loving aunt to us and a very welcoming great-aunt to our children. She lived by the sea and made all of us feel relaxed and very comfortable whenever we asked to spend a short holiday there; we were all very fond of her and when she was suffering her final illness Amba and her husband offered to take care of her in their own home, although sadly Uncle Bill had already arranged for her to go to a nursing home.

Mummy would never have given us up, though. She sold every possession that might fetch money, and her wedding ring went several times to what she called the 'pop shop': the pawnbroker's. We girls were her first priority; we were now her only valued possessions and she nurtured and cherished us for the rest of her life.

There came a day at Ireton Road when Amba and I were chasing each other around the furniture. This event comes to mind with absolute clarity.

Wearing only pink, fluffy, hand-knitted vests in a double-rib design, Amba and I, aged about three and four, ran around and around a large chair, each of us trying to catch the other, and squealing with excitement. Mummy was there, in the room, and I looked up at her each time I ran past her; it was something I would do habitually in the coming years. I needed to read the expression on her face because I could tell from that expression whether there was anything to be worried about or whether everything was all right. That day, something was definitely wrong!

Mummy was standing quite still and there was a blank expression on her hollow face; as she watched us, her blue eyes glazed with tears. She was wearing what looked like a print dress of some silky fabric which clung to her gaunt shoulders and she was standing between two strange men who were also watching us inertly and sadly. Although I was unable to understand its meaning, the tableau became imprinted on my mind throughout my childhood and years later, in my teens, I asked Mum about that memory. I could see that it pained her to talk about it, even then, but she explained that the men had come from the National Society for the Prevention of Cruelty to Children. The NSPCA had received a report from someone saying that we girls were all in need of care and protection.

No action was taken. Two robust little girls playing happily and one frail and undernourished mother must have been on the report. My poor mother suffered many painful experiences, but she always managed to summon up the strength to cope because of us. Usually when I think of her she is wearing a smile; it was her sword and shield.

Aunty Kitty helped. She was immensely supportive; she made clothes for us and sometimes discreetly left money on the table after a visit. One of my favourite dresses was made by her; it was knitted from crimson wool and had yellow embroidery at the neck and silver buttons like shining saucers. It was probably she who had made the fluffy pink vests; they were so furry that each time I wore mine a deposit of pink down filled my navel, which I would remove with fascination. Another dress of mine, made by Aunty Kitty, was of red and white check cotton, which I vandalised out of boredom one day. I sat down, wearing the dress, took a pair of scissors and cut slits upwards all around the hem. Mummy must have despaired! If only I had taken an interest in my father earlier, Aunty Kitty, as well as Mum, would have been able to tell me so much about our early years.

Mummy had already started to teach us how to accept our colour in the white society in which we lived; our father wasn't there to do so. Throughout our lives she stressed that we had nothing to be ashamed of; if people didn't like us because of the colour of our skin, then those people weren't worth knowing anyway, she explained. She vetted quite severely our two white suitors when we both started 'going steady', explaining that if children were born to us they might well be brown-skinned (both boyfriends were perfectly happy with that, anyway). She constantly told us how beautiful we both were. And this education had started when we were merely toddlers. One day she bought each of us a fairy doll, all complete with gossamer wings. Marjie's doll was pink-skinned with yellow hair; Amba's doll and mine were brown, with black hair.

I hated that fairy doll and, as young as I was – perhaps four or five – I found it intolerable that Mummy should point out, by giving me this black doll, that I was different from everyone else. I don't think I ever played with it. I was reminded of this one day about fifty years later. A black girl of about seven, with a white woman, boarded the bus I was travelling on; the girl was clutching to her chest a baby doll that was exactly the same colour as her own dark brown skin and it was clear that this was an adored possession. I now regret that I couldn't have loved my fairy doll as this child apparently loved her baby doll, but circumstances today are different from that time. Had there been at least one black adult, preferably more than one, in the family or among our circle of acquaintances, my view of the world would have been brighter.

It's quite amazing, really, that we never knew any other black people. After all, Britain has had black citizens for hundreds of years and during the 1930s there were many living here. But, oddly, none came our way. Amba and I were always the only children of our colour at all of the schools we attended and, for many years, in places of employment too.

Mummy was not only hardworking but she was also very prudent; she eked out what little money she earned and she never got into heavy debt. The one luxury she allowed herself, she told me, was two cigarettes a day. She later became a heavy smoker, although on health grounds she got away with it, luckily. It was not, then, common practice for cigarettes to have filter tips and Mum smoked Player's Navy Cut, a very strong brand, so that her poor, hard-worked, calloused fingers were stained with nicotine. This was, of course, before smoking was a known danger to health. It was still possible to smoke in designated areas on public transport – upstairs on a double-decker bus – and in the wintertime when we were young Mum always took us onto the upper deck if we travelled by bus because, she said, the smoky atmosphere up there would kill any germs! And if we were going somewhere by bus or tram without her, she never failed to instruct us beforehand to make sure we went upstairs.

By now the war was getting closer. The four of us had been on our own for three or four years and Mummy's health was being sorely tested because of all the work she was doing and the small amount of food she was allowing herself. Amba and I had started school at the age of three or four and because we had no shoes (something I don't remember and can scarcely believe) Amba recalls that Mummy *carried us both to school*. However, I do remember one day when, on a traffic island in the middle of Holloway Road, she tripped with us both in her arms. 'My babies!' she cried in alarm, but we were safe, although, curiously for one so young, her startled outburst embarrassed me. I seem to have spent my entire childhood in a state of embarrassment of one sort or another.

I say that I scarcely believe we had no shoes because even as a small child I thought of us as a cut above some of the impoverished little urchins about us, whose dirty, tide-marked faces looked so coarse and tired and their clothes so worn and shabby. I felt sorry for them and I placed ourselves, mentally, in a much higher social class. To me they were 'poor' children, and I never thought of my little family as poor; it was as though I instinctively felt that I was in the wrong environment. Yet when financial help was offered by the school authorities to some of our neighbours, Mum was often excluded, something she found a bit frustrating; we must have looked cleaner and more affluent than some of the other children, although we certainly weren't more affluent. The school we went to then was in Yerbury Road, and Amba triumphantly reported to Mummy one day that she had nits in her hair.

'Nits? Who says you've got nits?' Mummy wanted to know.

Apparently one of the teachers had examined Amba's hair. Mummy now did the same, and on finding Amba's hair perfectly clean, marched to the school the following day to enlighten the teacher that her daughter certainly did not have nits, but a little bit of scurf due, probably, to having her hair washed with laundry soap which was all that could be afforded – no delicate shampoos; they would have been far too costly for Mum's purse.

During this time Mummy was ill; she was lying on her back on a sofa and she was weeping. The tears flowed down the side of her face and it seemed to Amba, who was trying to comfort her, that they were trickling from her mother's ears.

'I'm going to smack Daddy when he comes home,' Amba cried.

She thought Mummy was dying and she raced to our grandmother's home several streets away.

'Come quickly! Mummy is dying,' she cried to Granny. 'Water is coming out of her ears!'

Six

In June 1939 Bruce Wendell was to be guest pianist with the Boston Symphony Orchestra (Howard Rye).

...Well, darling, I do hope you are settling down gradually to the little while of separation which is but the prelude, I hope with all my heart & soul, to my return to a much better position for you & all my other loved ones. I know that I have so much about me to distract & occupy my thoughts, that it is perhaps easier for me than for you; but, believe me, dearest, I miss you, & shall continue, I know, to miss you during these months. But they will soon pass, & we shall be together again, you & Amba & Anne & Margery & me. So chins up, old girl.

Now, I'm going to tea & a rest afterwards.

But we weren't to be together again; as it happened we were separated even farther. On the first day of September 1939 our poor, dear mum bade Marjie and Amba and me a tearful farewell as we were evacuated from London and the war. By now our father was safely in the United States and must have known that if we were still in London we faced danger and possible death. Even an event as momentous as a world war didn't prompt an enquiry from him. He may have been a man of 'singular personal charm', but he must have had a heart of granite and a conscience that had taken off never to return.

Some British children were evacuated to the United States; what an opportunity Bruce had then to redeem himself! But who knows now how far down the wrong road he had travelled by that time? He writes 'believe me, dearest'; if only that had been a possibility.

Mummy thought she had a solution to her problems. If she could help with the evacuation process she might be able to keep us all together. She offered her services to the appropriate authorities; she was capable of running a home for evacuees and asked to do so on condition that her own children be with her. Although her offer of help was accepted, the condition couldn't be guaranteed, so she withdrew and remained at her main job at the Whittington Hospital in Archway, north London. Our evacuation was an opportunity for her to have us safely cared for whilst she worked full-time in order to rebuild our lives.

So, less than four years after losing our father, we were parted from our mother. Marjie was eleven, Amba had had her seventh birthday only days earlier, and I was five-and-a-half. That morning Mum and, I think, Granny, stood outside Archway Underground Station with the other mothers, grandmothers and relatives as we all began our exodus. There was an air of uncertainty amongst the relatives whilst the teachers did their best to organise the children; there had, apparently, been rehearsals in the previous weeks and I have no doubt that some children assumed this was just another dummy run. More tears were in Mum's eyes and on her thin face a numb and worried expression; she hugged and kissed us and waved goodbye after promising to visit us *as soon as she knew where we were*! Because she could see our mother crying, Amba was very, very frightened. It must have been an alarming occasion for the parents as well as the children. No one seemed to know exactly where any of us were destined and the parents had to pin their hopes and trust on the teachers who accompanied the children. Barbra Streisand, in the song *The Way We Were*, sings: 'What's too painful to remember/We simply choose to forget.' Although this must have been as much a traumatic and momentous event for me as it was for my sisters, I don't remember the journey away from London; I chose to forget. I remember only the scene outside the Underground where there were huge crowds of people milling about. What I do recall, however, is Amba crying for days – I don't exaggerate – as we began our new lives in what seemed to me to be the other end of the world but which turned out to be only Bedfordshire. I'm sure she tried hard to be brave, but Amba couldn't hold back her grief; I can still see her sad little tear-stained face. She had soft, loose, brown curls, and even they looked damp. Marjie kept the three of us closely together throughout the train ride from King's Cross Station as we clutched our gas masks and bags of clothing along with the food that had been provided for the journey, digestive biscuits and condensed milk amongst other things.

We arrived at our destination, the small village of Clophill, where it was hoped good homes would be found for us. We were all put on display in the school hall and the villagers who had agreed to take on evacuees came to take their pick. That hall still has a firm place in my memory; it was there that, throughout the time we lived in Clophill, we had our lessons. Two classes were held simultaneously, each facing opposite ends of the hall. And it was also in that school hall that every so often our gas masks were checked and I experienced the fear of being suffocated as the masks, in place over our faces, were speedily tested, impeding the ability to breathe for a few seconds. From time to time extra filters, or whatever they were called, were added to the nose piece, or whatever that was called, making the masks ever heavier. But on that first day in the school hall Marjie, being older and more likely to be of practical help to her prospective fosterparents, was amongst the first to be chosen and taken away. Amba and I had lost our big sister as well as both our parents and Marjie had lost the two little sisters she had promised to take care of.

Later that day Amba and I were billeted together with two elderly ladies – or so they seemed to us then – who lived in a cottage opposite the school, but we were so young that the ladies returned us first thing the following morning like unwanted goods, saying they couldn't care for such small children.

So off we were shepherded to another home, this time with Mr and Mrs Izzard, a gentle farm worker and his kind wife who had two daughters of their own, Audrey, aged eighteen, and Cissie, eleven. When we arrived at their house Amba was still crying; she must have felt totally bereft. We were taken into the main living room that had a concealed staircase behind a latched, wooden door. A black cooking range and fire dominated the room; there was a large butler sink and, beneath the window overlooking the garden, a comfortable sofa. Amba and I sat on the sofa with the four concerned members of the family hovering anxiously over us, and in an effort to ease our unhappiness they brought out two toys: a fluffy dog and a doll. They decided that since I was the younger I should be offered the toys first and I chose the doll, but I felt desperately sorry for my heart-broken sister as she tried to sniff back her tears while she 'walked' the fluffy dog on the floor. I wished I had taken the dog so that she could cuddle the doll and perhaps get some sort of comfort. That memory still haunts me, and to this day I have rarely been so touched by the distress of a child.

We were asked to call Mr and Mrs Izzard 'mum' and 'dad', and although we complied with this request I felt disloyal to our own mother and tried never to refer to our foster parents in this way when Mummy was around. Our time with the Izzards was a happy enough one. We were given a part of the garden that we could use as our own and which contained a

Victoria plum tree, a delicious fruit that we were allowed to help ourselves to, and after we had settled in we played together in contentment. The family regularly bought a children's magazine called *Sunny Stories*, Enid Blyton tales,* which we read with eagerness and interest, and it was there that we first enjoyed going to proper school. We were provided with sweet little straw hats to wear for church, and our fostermother sewed new dresses for us. Further fresh experiences awaited us: there was gleaning in the fields when we collected corn or wheat left on the ground after harvesting, which would be put to good use in the kitchen. Also, I often watched as Mr Izzard attached a bucket to the end of a very long pole, straddled the top of a well in the garden and lowered several buckets, one at a time, deep down into what looked to me like a bottomless pit, collecting enough water to last the whole day. The buckets were then placed under the butler sink because the house had no water on tap. That well terrified me; it was not the stylised kind seen in fairy tales, the sort that has a little roof and a bucket hanging on a pulley activated by a revolving handle. It was merely a round hole covered with a large, flat, wooden lid which Mr Izzard removed carefully before placing one foot on either side of its gaping mouth. Although it was frightening I was also fascinated, in a self-terrifying sort of way, and felt compelled to watch the performance. Once or twice I stood beside Mr Izzard on the edge and looked wide-eyed down at the water far below. I don't like heights.

Because the house had no running water, the outside lavatory was halfway down the garden, which we thought was

---

* We read a lot of Enid Blyton stories and I later learned, through my research for this memoir, that Enid Blyton's second husband, Kenneth Darrell Waters, had been a contemporary of Bruce Wendell at Keble College; he was admitted in 1911, a year after Bruce. Such a small world!

very strange and rather frightening in the dark, and we didn't like using it in cold weather. Mr Izzard had the unpleasant job of emptying and cleaning the lavatory. We had a regular 'bath night' when a long, grey galvanised tub was removed from where it hung outside, brought into the main living room and placed in front of the cooking range. Being the smallest I was usually bathed first. One day Mrs Izzard decided it would improve the appearance of the tub if she painted its inside. She set to, and left the white paint to dry for a day or two.

When next bath night came around, warm water was poured into the tub and I stepped in and sat down, but it soon became apparent that the white paint had not been given long enough to dry hard. When I stood up my bottom, back, arms and legs were daubed with the white paint! I know I wished my skin was lighter in colour, but not in this way! Everyone was shocked, but we could also see the funny side of the situation.

I was placed across Mrs Izzard's lap and, with a cloth soaked in turpentine, she rubbed at my little brown bum until all the paint was removed. Then she started on the rest of me. Goodness knows what effect it had on my skin and I expect I had to have another wash of some kind in order to remove the turpentine. The whole family observed the scene, though, with amused interest. How did the others get bathed that week, I wonder? I don't know what happened to the tub; it probably needed to be replaced.

The garden itself seemed a magic place and was something quite unfamiliar to us. It was very long and planted with flowers, fruit and vegetables and ran down to the River Flit. Although the river wasn't very deep or wide we were, naturally, banned from going too near, but we were able to experience a certain enchantment while sitting beside the trickling water as we sat reading on warm sunny days. I don't think that the Izzards had any pets, but there were several geese roaming around and a very big gooseberry bush grew about halfway down the garden. The Izzards allowed us to eat the fruit if we wanted to and it was with a shock one day that I heard someone say that they must have been called gooseberries because geese liked to eat them; apparently we'd almost stripped the bush bare and the poor geese got the blame!

It was the first time I had seen such a profusion of daffodils; in spring the entire front part of the garden was brilliant with their colour and villagers came to buy them for one penny each, or one shilling (5p) a dozen. Amba and I played happily together – it was a blessing that we were never parted. We were very innovative and imaginative in our play. There had been some construction work started in part of the garden that had been interrupted by the outbreak of the war; a building stood incomplete with unsmoothed, solidified cement oozing from between some of the red bricks. We took some of the broken bricks that were lying around, rubbed them together in order to make a reddish powder, then mixed the powder with water. The paste which resulted from this procedure we then packed into small jars or pots that we stacked together and put into our store of playtime 'food'; they became fish and meat paste. Sometimes we would mix together sand and earth; this was our recipe for fruit cake. On one occasion I took a brick which was too large for me to handle and attempted to hurl it to the ground in order to break it into smaller bits but accidentally hit Amba hard on the head. Goodness, how she bawled; it must have been a forceful blow and I was very afraid that I'd hurt her badly, but fortunately she was all right after a bit of comforting.

We were quite happy with the Izzards and Mrs Izzard was such a caring woman that she even visited us years later at our very last billet. We spoke in a completely different accent to the villagers and I made a determined effort to copy their dialect and Amba must have done the same, so that our London voices became country burrs, which greatly amused Mum.

Cissie, the only surviving member of the four Izzards we knew, gives me the impression that they were happy to take care of us and to give us some of the love and affection that we were missing away from home. They always made Mummy very welcome when she visited us and sent her home with flowers and home-grown vegetables. I don't know why we were moved from Clophill, but Cissie believes that her mother became unwell. Later the Izzards had a son, Brian, so that may have been the reason we had to go. I met Brian at Cissie's home and he told me that the family often spoke of their little evacuees. However, after leaving Clophill our circumstances seemed to take a turn for the worse with one or two short periods of respite.

Whilst some London evacuees enjoyed the lives they led in the country, for some the experience was hateful, and Amba and I found ourselves in this second category upon leaving the Izzards. The next billet was with another farm worker in a village called Tingrith, not far from Clophill. He had a wife and, again, two daughters, although I remember nothing of the girls – my memory of evacuation seems to be very selective. This second home was somewhat more modern than the Izzards'. For instance, the Smiths had a properly plumbed kitchen with running water and a coal-heated washing boiler. This kitchen was separate from but adjoining the living room which, in turn, led to a front door (never used) through a small hallway with a staircase to the bedrooms. Mr Smith – that was the family name – wore black leather gaiters, which we'd never seen before, and when he returned from the fields in the evenings he would reach up to a shelf in the kitchen and take down a jam jar that contained cold tea which his wife had placed there, and he would take a long drink from the jar. It looked absolutely delicious; I think it really was tea and not beer or some other alcoholic beverage.

Unhappily for us, at this billet we were very inadequately fed and clothed to the point where we stole food and ate berries, nuts, acorns and even leaves from the hedgerows. It seems to me now that we always wore summer clothes despite a severe winter. We had to walk through the snow to school, probably about a mile away, wearing white sandals, and Amba suffered badly from broken chilblains that scarred her feet permanently. The Smiths accused us of being vain and removed every mirror in the house so that we couldn't admire ourselves, an unjust indictment that puzzled and aggrieved us both. Perhaps we were a bit prettier than the two Smith daughters, causing their parents to be jealous; who knows the reason? Strangely, though, Mrs Smith made us some nice little frocks, blue with pink flowers, although when we were sent to our next billet the frocks didn't go with us. I don't think we were there for long. On Sunday evenings we all went on a 'pub crawl'. Mr and Mrs Smith went into each public house on the route and bought us children, who had to sit outside on the front step, a soft drink and an arrowroot biscuit; another novelty. Amba and I found this a strange and boring recreation, but at least we got something to eat along the way.

Apart from mealtimes, the pub crawl was the only interaction we had with the Smith family and we were invariably isolated from everyone else, never having any contact outside of school with any other children, the two Smith girls in the house or any other adults. After school, whatever the weather, we played in a shed at the end of the long vegetable garden. Someone had given us lengths of green cloth and these we draped over our heads, tied a string around our necks and pretended they were beautiful hooded cloaks. A small black kitten joined us in the shed and we were distressed to see, one day, that it couldn't stand; it kept falling over and each time it did so we picked it up and placed it back on its feet. Then it would totter around in a half-circle and fall again. The poor thing must have suffered a stroke, I realised years later, and we were very upset about the little creature's condition. It died, of course.

Mummy came to see us and was shocked at how thin we had become. At the end of the lane where we were living was a tree that Amba and I thought was magic. It had a scar at the base of its trunk that, with a bit of imagination, could have been a doorway. We had read *The Faraway Tree* by Enid Blyton; this was our Faraway Tree. If we were very good, we might one day be able to open the door and enter an enchanted world. Mummy and I were sitting beneath the Faraway Tree. She took one of my arms and examined it.

'You look very thin,' she observed, with some alarm.

I withdrew my arm immediately, sensing her anxiety, and tried to assure her, with an instinct common to children wishing to protect their parents from worry, that we were both fine.

But a short while after this our fosterparents found out that we had stolen and eaten almost their entire crop of pears which had been stored in the shed where we played. There was a dog kennel in the shed and we discovered that if we climbed up on to its roof after placing it on a chair, one of us was tall enough to reach into the fruit boxes stacked on the rafters. We almost got caught on an earlier occasion when we were sitting reading, dressed in our green 'cloaks' and with our backs against sacks of vegetables, contentedly tucking into our latest ill-gotten gains. We heard someone coming down the garden and hastily pushed the evidence behind us, hoping for the best. We got away with it that time, and I have to smile now when I think of the shock those unkind people must have had when they discovered they had no pears to take them through the next season. We must have made a regular habit of eating the pears because even we were surprised at how few were left. We had even polished off the cores and stalks, leaving no evidence.

This family fed us in the most bizarre way; for breakfast they would eat cereals – Shredded Wheat, as I recall – but Amba and I were served with only the crumbs from the bottom of the box; because it was wartime, the cereal box contained no inner bag as is the case today and the contents must have been easily broken, which may have been to our advantage. For the main midday meal Amba and I had the remains of yesterday's pudding to start with whilst our fosterfamily ate a hearty meat dish, and then we all ate today's pudding afterwards. It took me years to get out of the habit of licking a finger, then picking up and eating every last crumb left on my plate. There would have been no need to wash any plate I had used for a meal! I think these people must have agreed to take evacuees in order to get extra food rations, which they kept for themselves. Most of the villagers seemed to resent the evacuee children's presence, calling us 'dirty little Londoners', and Mr and Mrs Smith described us as little savages because on one occasion, whilst eating rice pudding, I waved my spoon and accidentally showered grains of rice over the table and on Amba, which they were convinced I had done on purpose, something hardly likely because I would have wanted to eat every last morsel. However, I can't recall that they ever laid a hand on us, not even when the Great Pears Robbery came to light.

Mummy was sent for! Amba and I stood outside the little farm-worker's cottage watching anxiously as she strode with fierce determination past the Faraway Tree and along the lane towards us. We were ashamed to have given her cause for worry and for having disgraced her, and were afraid of how cross she would be with us. But to our astonishment, far from being angry with us, she was furious with our fosterparents who had come outside to wait with us.

'Thieving?' Mummy exclaimed. 'My girls thieving? Look at them! No wonder they've been thieving! Can't you see they're starving?' And then she stooped, gathered us both into her loving arms and gave us long and warm reassuring hugs and kisses.

She insisted we were moved immediately and she must have made the necessary arrangements before coming to Tingrith that day. She demanded that our possessions be fetched from the house straight away, and we set off once again with our few clothes, gas masks, identity cards and ration books.

I wonder if the mirrors were ever replaced.

Each move to a new home was carried out by the same plump, bowler-hatted billeting officer who, when it was just the three of us, always sat Amba on the back seat and me in the front passenger seat so that he could put his left hand down inside the back of my knickers and fondle my bottom as we drove in his car. We hated that man and Amba never forgot his name: Mr Johnson.

Seven

*Last night I played a bit. The piano in the Music Room
is a Grotrian-Steinweg Grand, rather the worse for
sea-air & wear, but quite playable. Zorina would not be
satisfied until she asked the purser to let me play a
while instead of the band, so I played the Beethoven
Rondo in G & the Scherzo from the Chopin Sonata. The
Captain & Officers & their parties applauded very
much, & off I went to bed, satisfied that the fingers
were in working order. They wanted Z to sing but she
would not.*

We were packed off to a hostel in the high street of a large
market town, which was run by a matron and nurse. It was
what I imagine a boarding-school residence would be like.
Because the large house had a semi-basement, the protective
railings had not been soldered off and sent away to help the
war effort, as had many ornamental iron railings, and the front
door was reached by six or seven stone steps. It was an elegant
building with bow windows onto the street and it later became
an antique shop (I returned to have a look round the town in
the 1970s – not so much a sentimental journey as one born of
curiosity). There were six girls, including us, and it was great;
the matron and nurse were strict, but we didn't mind that; you
know where you are with strict. We each had to help with
washing- and wiping-up the dishes and our meals were
carefully prepared with rations fairly shared. Each teatime we

first had a slice of bread and margarine, then a couple of slices of bread and Canadian strawberry jam (we knew it was from Canada because the label on the jar bore a picture of the maple leaf) and we were required to eat in silence at every meal. After Sunday school each week, we were told to stay together and to take a walk until midday, which was boring, especially in cold weather; there wasn't much of interest in the town on a Sunday. It would have been different in midweek when the cattle market arrived. That was fascinating and exciting; I often stood for ages in silent awe, regardless of weather conditions, watching the cows being herded from pen to truck up a wooden ridged ramp, their bony hooves slipping on smelly muck before a somewhat unsafe-looking little wooden gate was snapped across to lock them in. But on Sundays the town was featureless with all the shops closed; we all waited impatiently for the Town Hall clock to strike twelve times and then hurried back to the hostel for what was a nourishing lunch (or dinner, as it was probably called). We spent a Christmas there and I, who no longer believed in Father Christmas, had my faith in him restored.

The six of us came down on Christmas morning after all feeling extremely disappointed that there had been no presents by our beds. We were called into the sitting room where Matron and Nurse were standing beside a small pile of Christmas gifts. They greeted us.

'Happy Christmas,' we all replied.

'Girls,' Matron said cheerily, 'look what I discovered on the mantelpiece.'

In her hand she held a paper doily with red writing on.

'Father Christmas,' she explained, 'has left a letter for you.'

She began to read it and, although I can't recall the message word for word, it went something like: 'Dear boys and girls – no, that's not right. Dear girls, I was so late – no, I should say, so early – or was it late? – with my rounds last night – or was it this morning? – that I didn't have time to bring each of you your gifts. So forgive me; I left them all here so that Matron could hand them to you.' It was signed 'Father Christmas.'

We all read the untidy handwriting on the doily. It had to be true; there was a Father Christmas or he could not have left us a message. I would believe in him for ever, I told myself.

This home was exactly the kind of place that Mummy had hoped to be able to run, so long as she had her daughters with her, and knowing how competent she was, she would have made a success of it. It would have been ideal and would have prevented a lot of misery and worry. However, this hostel was a short-stay billet where girls were housed until a more permanent home could be found, although I'd have been perfectly happy to stay there for the duration of the war.

So a little while later we were moved across the road to live with Mr Ashdown and his French wife; we understood that they had met during the first world war when, presumably, Mr Ashdown was a soldier in France. There we were taken good care of and Mrs Ashdown fed us very differently from our last permanent billet. The food was delicious and we were served with home-made soup, which was something of a novelty for us. The couple, a solemn pair who had no children, kept chickens and rabbits in the back yard like many other families did during the war in order to provide extra meat and eggs. They hardly ever spoke to us and talked to each other in French. Was Mr Ashdown retired, or was he employed? The everyday details of life there are lost to me and I can't even recall what either of the two looked like. Maybe that's a good thing; at least I don't have memories of horrible experiences.

Theirs was a dark little house, but not unpleasant; the front door led directly from the outside pavement into the one living room and the kitchen extended into the back yard. Like the Izzards' house in Clophill, the stairs were hidden behind a wooden door in the main room. Again, I have no idea how long we stayed with these people; we had been with the Izzards at least a year, and with the Smiths maybe six months, and I know that I was seven when we arrived at our next and last billet so perhaps we were with the Ashdowns for about another six months. We had no complaints there. Well, perhaps there was one thing we didn't like, but it was no one's fault.

A female visitor called frequently, usually on a Sunday, to join us for a meal. I don't know what her relationship to our fosterparents was and I couldn't determine her age. She always wore a black, brimmed hat and the heavy black veil covering her face was held firmly under the chin and tied at the back of her head. When the veil and hat were removed the most frightful wound was exposed on her left cheek. It was an open sore covering the whole of that side of her face and covered with thick white powder which, with the movement of her face as she spoke, cracked to reveal lines of raw, red flesh. The wound smelled awful, and we understood (but we may have made this bit up) that as it grew larger and eventually reached her eye, she would die! It was almost touching her eye already and the lower lid was dragged down, cruelly exposing its bright red lining. She must have been in much discomfort or even severe pain, and Amba and I felt really sorry for this poor woman who must have had some form of skin cancer or an incurable ulcer, but we didn't like sitting at table with her. It was another of those morbidly fascinating sights, although I did try not to stare at her; I knew what it was like to be stared at.

After leaving the Ashdowns, we spent the remainder of the war years at the other end of the same town with a large, extended family, sometimes living in the matriarch's house, sometimes with one of her married daughters, and usually separated at nights.

So, as can be imagined, there had been several new schools for us to brave. The first day was always something of an ordeal because the rest of the children had never before seen anyone like Amba and me and we were asked questions that became repetitive and tedious, such as 'Are you the same colour all over?' or 'How do you know when you're dirty?' And to the endless 'Where do you come from?' I always answered firmly, 'London', although I was not assertive enough to leave the question mark hanging there and usually qualified my response with, 'But my father came from the West Indies.' Even grown-ups made stupid remarks such as 'Is it warm enough for you?' if the sun was shining brightly or 'I expect you don't like the cold' in winter time. As it happens, Amba is very uncomfortable in hot weather, even in our temperate English climate. Such silly remarks and thoughtless interrogation emphasised our isolation, our uniqueness. Our father had left England because he believed himself to be the victim of racial prejudice, but his appearance was far less uncommon in his environment than Amba's and mine were in ours. At least he had known, and mingled with, other black people here. In the interview 'Oxford in My Time' in the *Georgetown Daily Chronicle* mentioned earlier, Bruce includes a piece about other black scholars at Oxford, and I include it here to illustrate my point:

PLATO HIS FAVOURITE

Plato was my favourite then, and H.A. Lowe, a Barbados scholar, and I used to go for long walks, conversing in Platonic prose.

Barbados sent up some very brilliant scholars to Oxford then and, I believe, still continues to do so. Lowe won a

---

classical scholarship at Hertford College with a piece of Greek prose so perfect that the examiners commented that it might well have been a lost fragment of Thucydides. ...C.H. Clarke, another excessively brilliant Barbados scholar, was at Oxford in my time. He and Hutton-Mills, a West African from Cambridge who used to come over to Oxford to see Clarke, liked to hear me play, and so they had a piano placed in Clarke's room so that whenever I went in to see them they could hear me. There was another West Indian, by name Mercier, from Jamaica, a Rhodes scholar, a most charming and cultured fellow, and a great cricketer, who nearly got his blue. Then there were the two Newsams from Barbados, and Nethersole from Jamaica. Another great personality was Sukuna, the son of a Fijian chief, who had a very distinguished war career.

However, there were also compensations for us once we became established and comfortable in our new schools. We were always popular with other children and made friends easily. One boy of my age, about nine, whose name was Dickie and who always seemed to sport a snotty nose, declared his undying love for me and one day, to my horror, when a group of us were playing Off Ground Touch, he managed to kiss my cheek, snot and all!

The school playground had a brick, covered shelter, and around the three inside walls stretched a wooden bench. The object of Off Ground Touch was to make sure your feet were not on the ground otherwise whoever was 'It' could catch you, but you had to keep moving and stay in the chase. I had run into the shelter and jumped up onto the bench when suddenly Dickie joined me and placed the kiss on my cheek. Dear Dickie – he was probably quite a sweetie really. Several of us were up for the cane one day; boys first. We stood there in line and Dickie stoically took his punishment. When it was my turn he was transformed into my knight in shining armour. He lifted his chin; 'I'll take hers, sir,' he said, firmly and courageously, holding out his palm. To my disappointment, though, he wasn't allowed to take mine; I had to take my own caning on the hand. Although I have never forgotten Dickie, I can't remember whether he was an evacuee or a local.

There was a teacher who wore a brown tweed suit whose name I don't recall. He was a very likeable and jovial man who made classes and lessons fascinating because he filled them with fun. I think that during the war years teachers taught multiple subjects; there would have been a shortage of teaching staff then and I think that this genial, tweed-suited teacher taught Maths and English and, also, Scripture. One of his remarks I shall always remember; it was a Bible lesson and he was telling us the story of Joshua. As he strode theatrically around the front of the class he enunciated at the top of his voice, 'Joshua, Joshua. Nicer than lemon squash, you are.' This I found wonderfully amusing; I thought he'd made it up on the spur of the moment but later found out that it was part of an old Music Hall song. At that time Amba and I were both in the same class for some unknown reason; we were diligent pupils and this teacher rewarded us with a penny each on more than one occasion because we had the best handwriting in the class.

So, we were moved from the Ashdowns – I don't know why – and when we arrived at our last billet with the detested Mr Johnson we were shown into the big, rather cluttered living room, which featured a huge fireplace. Taking up the centre of the room was a very large dining table (always covered with a thick cloth) with chairs around it, a few armchairs had been placed against the walls and a big radio, from which the family could hear the war news, stood on a shelf beside the fireplace. The linoleum-covered floor had dull, uninteresting rugs spread around the table. Outside, through a french door, was a small concrete yard; we never went out there and I can't recall that the door was ever opened. A tiny room, opposite the fireplace, led off the main one; it was the kitchen – no more than a scullery really; it would have been possible to reach every necessary utensil and piece of equipment in that minuscule room without moving your feet an inch in any direction. Into this tiny kitchen was crammed not only a stove and sink, but also a copper where the laundry was washed and boiled.

When we arrived, lolling in one of the armchairs sprawled a dark haired, blue-eyed, five-year-old girl, two years younger than me, and as Mr Johnson, Amba and I came into the room she looked us up and down with a sly sneer on her face. I took an instant dislike to her. I shall call her Rose.

Then, as if she were choosing a new plaything for herself, or perhaps a hair ribbon, she announced condescendingly to her grandmother who was to be our fostermother for the remainder of the war, 'I like the little one, Gran.'

Oh do you? Well, I don't like you, I thought.

Gran, or Granny as we were told to call her, was standing behind Rose. A thick-set, heavy-jowled woman of about fifty with frizzy grey hair and a mouth like a letter box, she had five evacuees, including us, one or two regular fosterchildren and several lodgers, one of whom was a young woman who had been billeted there by the Meteorological Office. Amba and I later realised that apart from two of the other evacuees this young woman was the only one in the entire household who seemed to have any intelligence, although we had very little to do with her other than sharing the same table at meal times. And what horrible meals they were usually. The other evacuees were two boys, both Johns and older than us, and one sixteen-year-old girl whose name I don't remember. Why a sixteen-year-old should still have been an evacuee I can't imagine; had I reached that age and the war had still not been won I would have cleared off to my own home *tout de suite* or gone anywhere away from that family, but I didn't know her circumstances. There were probably more residents. I can't remember all of them; the large house was always full. Granny also had four daughters and a son. However, she didn't have a husband; we learned that he had left her years earlier – and who could blame him?

The family were Salvationists and they all lived in the same town except for the eldest daughter, who had moved with her husband and family to a neighbouring village and who we rarely met; the family appeared to think she had married above herself, and I must say that on the one occasion that we were taken to see her she did strike me as being rather grand.

Whilst billeted with this family we took most of our meals at Granny's house, but our nights were usually spent in the homes of the older daughters. Amba slept most of the time in the house of the second eldest daughter, who I shall refer to as Flo; she was a thin, dark-haired woman, probably in her thirties, whose husband was not in the forces, being engaged on war work. These were the parents of Rose, and Rose liked to tell lies about us in order to get Amba and me in trouble. She would report fictitious deeds or remarks to Granny, who would give us a smack round the head or a spiteful pinch on the cheek. When the war ends, I resolved, I'm going to invite Rose to stay with us in London, and then I'll get her in trouble and she'll be punished (something that never happened, of course; in any case, Mum wouldn't have hit her). Amba dreaded breakfast at this house. The family had a lodger, and during the morning meal he would ask the husband what sort of sexual activity had taken place the night before. Graphic descriptions were given, worrying and embarrassing Amba acutely.

Flo was a mean and unkind woman; she, along with her mother, sisters and brother, wore her Salvation Army uniform with pride; the crest with the words 'Blood and Fire' embroidered across the front of the scarlet vest peeked out through the front opening of her uniform, which was topped by the demure bonnet fastened with a large bow on the left side; and, of course, she attended all the services. But Amba and I could never have described her as God-fearing or Christian. Her husband was not a Salvationist; we learned that he had attended the meetings with Flo just long enough to court her, but after they married he became what was called 'a backslider'.

Across the road from Flo's house was a corner shop, a small grocer's, that sold really scrumptious fruit tarts; Flo would buy these tarts and give them to Rose, making it quite plain that they 'were not for her' – meaning not for Amba. And in the morning she would sometimes sneak up to the room where Rose and Amba slept and she would whisper to Rose that it was time to wake up and get ready for school, adding 'Leave her there!' so that Amba might be late for school, not realising, because she was just as dim and stupid as the rest of her family, that Amba was already awake and would get herself dressed as soon as the two of them had left the room. Can it be wondered that we learned to loathe this hypocritical and cruel family who showed the world a holier-than-thou face and who were anything but?

I was placed with the third eldest daughter, whose husband was a soldier fighting in Italy. She resembled her older sisters in colouring and stature; all had the same dark hair and slim build and all three are now faceless in my mind. The two youngest siblings were very different in appearance from the others and I now wonder whether they had had a different father. The son was, I would guess, in his mid-twenties; an extremely tall and thin man with red hair. I have no idea why he wasn't in one of the armed forces because he wasn't engaged on war work; he was a very simple man, but a kind one with whom we had very few dealings (although after the war, when he married, he and his young wife came to London to stay with us for a few days in our new flat and they went to the theatre to see the musical *Bless the Bride*). It soon came to our attention that the entire family was simple-minded. The youngest daughter, who I shall call Gladys, was eighteen, and we came to loathe her for reasons I come to later. Gladys looked very much like her mother; she was plump with coarse, frizzy, chestnut-coloured hair, which she wore in an upswept style, and it was her habit to sit in an ungainly and undignified way, her legs sprawled apart, prompting coarse remarks and much sniggering from the two Johns, who were about thirteen or fourteen, which she seemed to enjoy and to encourage.

We did see each other every day, however, and Amba, who was far more badly affected than I by those years and who seemed to get more thwacks about the head, was always quick to defend me if I got a beating or was unfairly criticised. We frequently got a clip round the ear and often we didn't know why. Every bit of confidence was knocked out of us; every ounce demolished, and although I subsequently recovered fairly quickly from the effects of our life with this family, Amba was not to become as carefree as I later did; she became a worrier in her adult years and was often unduly anxious about matters that others might find inconsequential.

One day the Salvation Army Captain visited the house and sat me on his lap.

'That girl will grow up to be a Jezebel,' declared Granny, spitefully.

Amba pounced on this; she knew that Jezebel was said to have been a very wicked woman. She was brave enough to shout her condemnation at our fostermother, telling her to leave me alone. She probably earned herself a slap after the Captain had left the house. This family professed to be deeply religious, but living with them gave us our first introduction to hypocrisy of the worst kind.

Eight

*The other passengers are gradually thawing. Z was
placed at the ship's doctor's table, there being only one
vacant place there. I told the Chief Steward that I did
not wish to sit with any strangers who might not want
me with them; so I sit in great state on my own. There
are others, I notice, who like their own company. But is
is rather amusing how people, & some of the nicest
passengers, gradually are going out of their way to talk
to me.*

So Bruce, now on board ship, was in the same situation as
when at Oxford and the Officers' Training Corps; he was fully
aware that some strangers might not want him with them,
presumably based on the colour of his skin, and so he put
himself in charge of the matter in order to avoid humiliation
by informing the chief steward that he would sit alone. We
who now live in a time of equal opportunities will recognise
such intolerance as totally unjustifiable. There were, though,
black entertainers in the 1930s who *were* accepted into white
high society, but probably only when they were successful and
famous. It makes me wonder how Bruce would have helped
his daughters to overcome any potential racism and indignity
they might have encountered in their lives; would it be by
example or by instruction? From what I have read about my
father, I can tell that he was deeply hurt at the racist treatment
he received from some people in England; it would almost

have been better (all round) had he not won the scholarship to Oxford.

So, here we were at what would be our last billet and where we would stay for the four final years of the war, and whilst living with these so-called pious Salvationists I got to learn the true and deep meaning of the word 'disappointment'. I likened it to an almost unbearable ache in the stomach, made worse by the fact that I daren't shed tears; to do so would have invited punishment – 'I'll give you something to cry about.' Life for me had now become a series of such bitter disappointments; a life that was a far cry from what our father's young existence must have been. Despite it all, though, we remained reasonably well behaved and were careful, intuitively, not to cause our mum any further heartache. She came to see us as often as she could, almost always on a Sunday – possibly the one day of the week when she wasn't carrying out her duties at the hospital – and sometimes, because Marjie had been returned to London, she brought our big sister or raven-haired, smiling Aunt Emily or even rarer, Aunty Kitty, with her; they were always welcome surprises.

Yet Amba and I never told each other, or anyone, about the sexual abuse each of us suffered at the hands of members of that family, male and female; the shame we felt made us keep the obscene behaviour secret even from each other; there was no one we could tell, and who would have believed us, anyway? God-fearing Salvationists assaulting small children? Unheard of! A lot of children suffered in the same way, I later discovered, but I doubt whether many spoke up about it at the time. Although this behaviour was totally repulsive and loathsome to us and we knew that it was wrong, we didn't know how to be other than obedient and the situation was just one of the many things we hated about living with these people. It was not until we were back home in London that it was talked about, and then only between the two of us. Our mother never knew, and I'm glad she didn't. I'm not sure that we even told Marjie.

I remember very little about the bedrooms where we slept whilst we were evacuated. I know that with the Izzards' I slept on a folding canvas camp bed but only because one night I fell out of it. Apart from that incident the bedrooms and beds of that period have almost all been erased from my mind. The conspicuous exception to this mental obliteration concerns our last billet. Sometimes we slept at Granny's house, and when that happened one of us shared the eighteen year-old Gladys's bed. On those occasions I was invariably woken during the night by her using one of my fingers for the purpose of masturbation. Of course I didn't at that time know what masturbation was; I knew neither the word nor the deed. All my child's mind could take in was that Gladys was doing something very 'rude'. Horrified and repulsed by this activity, I pretended to remain asleep but, revoltingly, she would then wipe my finger on her pubic hair and push her own finger into me, whispering, 'Do you like it? It's nice, isn't it?' She was vile.

I wouldn't have been able to think of anything I liked less or that I found more disgusting. Not only did it hurt, but I experienced an instinctive revulsion, mixed with fear, of something I couldn't understand, and I was also confused as to why her body was so different from my own. The reason for this was, of course, because I hadn't yet reached puberty. Although I tried to withdraw from her loathsome embrace, she persevered, although I don't know whether she got any gratification from this abhorrent behaviour. The same thing happened to Amba when she was sleeping there.

I said to Amba one day when we were back home in London, 'I hated Gladys.'

'So did I,' she replied. 'She used to do horrible things to me.'

'And to me,' I said.

And then we realised we'd both been subjected to abuse and told each other, for the first time, about the ordeals we'd suffered.

The daughter I lived with – I'll call her Poppy – was kind enough to me but again she was very dim-witted, and one day she received a letter from her husband telling her that he was to be discharged from the army because he had been injured. There was a visitor in another part of the house at the time and as she sat in the kitchen reading the letter, Poppy called out to her, 'Mollie, what's VD?'

I piped up, 'Venereal disease!'

'You naughty girl,' came the chastisement. 'You shouldn't be listening to our conversation.' And I was sent away.

I didn't understand; what had I done wrong now? Although I didn't have a clue as to what venereal disease might be, I could, and did, read adequately, unlike this idiotic family, and I learned from my reading. I had joined the local library and as well as books I absorbed anything and everything – labels on jars of jam and bottles of sauce, bus tickets, advertisements, all the notices displayed outside the local cinema – and I had seen posters on the fronts of buses: a baby's face with the shadow of the letters VD across it and the words 'Venereal Disease Kills'. When I had called out the answer to the question I even mispronounced it, placing the stress on the third syllable of 'venereal', and I thought I was being helpful so that Poppy's angry reaction hit me forcefully and painfully. It was yet another deep disappointment. It seemed I could do nothing to please.

Poppy had no children, but I was told that earlier she had had a baby that had died or been stillborn. Poppy lived in a small house with a tiny yet tidy kitchen and a living room with a large dining table and chairs and a sofa; on the wall facing the fireplace hung a huge framed print of Millais's *Bubbles*, a painting used in a Pear's Soap advertisement and, tucked into one corner of its enormous gilt frame was a postcard depicting the advertisement with a copy of the same painting.

Sometimes it would be Poppy's task to count the collection money from the Salvation Army open air meetings and I loved to help with that; we would heap up the pennies and halfpennies into piles representing shillings and the silver coins into pounds. There was never paper money to count.

Again, the stairs to the upper floor were hidden behind a latched door in the living room and they led up to two bedrooms although Poppy and I shared a large double bed in the front. The wardrobe in this room was one of the biggest I'd ever seen and there was hardly room to move round the bed, which was also very large and high; it took quite an effort to climb up on to it. There was another equally huge wardrobe in the back room too, and I wondered how on earth these enormous pieces of furniture had been carried up the narrow staircase; probably in sections, I supposed. Poppy would entertain me sometimes by showing me the lingerie she had earlier collected for her trousseau and I thought some of her silk and satin nightdresses were so lovely they could have been worn as evening gowns. She was a very plain woman in her late twenties and it surprised me to see that she had such glamorous underwear. She would also show me the baby clothes still preserved with loving care in the drawers.

There was no bathroom in this funny little house although there was in Granny's large house; but I can't remember ever using the bath at Granny's. At Poppy's house, though, there was a similar arrangement to the one at Clophill; a long galvanised bath would be brought into the kitchen and filled with hot water where I would scrub myself. And when I say hot water, I mean *hot* water. Poppy would expect me to get into the tub with water at the highest temperature I could possibly endure because she needed it to be warm enough for her own bath afterwards. I used to lower myself into the water as gently and slowly as I could, adjusting myself to the ferocious heat which made the colour of my skin change to a distinctive pinkish tan. For the rest of my life I would be able to tolerate very hot baths. It was in that little kitchen that I experienced one of the most delicious meals I ever ate with this family. Poppy had acquired from a neighbour a large quantity of spanish onions; during wartime when practically everything was rationed, an offer of any food was never refused. Poppy sliced the onions and fried them slowly; the aroma was mouth-watering and eventually a huge plateful was placed in front of me; those were the tastiest onions I'd ever eaten.

In due time the husband – I'll name him Stan – arrived back home. On the day of his return we children had all been taken on a Sunday School day trip and Poppy was one of the adults accompanying us. We arrived back at Granny's house in the late afternoon, all weary and dishevelled, and Granny opened the door between the living room and hall where we were taking off our clothes, and announced that Stan was back. I was excited at the prospect of meeting him – he had been talked about a lot and described as handsome and I thought he would be interesting, especially as he played the trumpet in the Salvation Army band, we were told – so I glanced back at Poppy with a smile; I was glad for her. To my surprise she looked startled and shy and, blushing, put a hand to her head and patted at her untidy hair. Then she held back a moment or two before shyly going in to hug him because he didn't come out of the room to greet her; he remained sitting in a chair and the rest of us all looked on at their reunion. I can see now how self-conscious and bashful Poppy must have felt, although at the time I couldn't understand her reaction.

So, because Stan would be sharing his wife's bed in my place, I was to sleep on the sofa downstairs in their home.

One night I had a bad dream and cried out and Stan came down ostensibly to see what was the matter. As he stepped through the door from the stairs I could see that he had purposely left his pyjamas gaping at the front, exposing his hideous penis, and that he was leering at me. I was seven or eight and his behaviour shocked me; it was like receiving a physical blow. Scared by this horrible display I tried to pretend I hadn't noticed, but I have no doubt that he enjoyed my fear. And that was only the first time it happened. This couple, too, didn't care how they behaved in front of a child. At breakfast Stan would put his hand up under Poppy's dress and they'd both giggle. I longed to escape this awful family. Some of our friends who were evacuees ran away back to London but they were always caught at King's Cross station and returned. Amba and I never had the courage to run away, mainly, I think, because it would have been too worrying for Mum.

Sometimes, when sleeping together at Granny's house, Amba and I were still awake when she came to bed. The bedroom where we slept in her house was a very big one and contained two – or maybe three – double beds; we never had the luxury of sleeping alone and we seemed not to have a bed of our own, but slept wherever we were told to. It was like Musical Beds. On more than one occasion Granny came into the room thinking we were asleep and knelt to say her prayers aloud after removing her flesh-pink laced corsets (I thought that when we grew up it would be compulsory for us also to wear ugly flesh-pink brassieres and corsets and I dreaded becoming an adult, especially since this unpleasant pinkness wasn't flesh-coloured for the likes of me). She bowed her head over her double chin and thick neck, her once-red hair partly concealed under a silver helmet of Dinky curlers tightly twisted there to maintain the grey frizz that peeked out from under her Salvation Army bonnet, and uttered her prayers.

There was one plea she often offered up fervently. It was, 'And oh God! Make Jim love me. Make Jim love me.'

Jim (which is not his real name) was a member of the Salvationist congregation and was a married man with a family who, by the way, was carrying on with Gladys, we later learned. Amba and I giggled about Granny's prayer, not realising how sinful it would appear to her God. Another of her favourite remarks was, 'When I reach the Pearly Gates, St Peter will say to me, "Come on in, Mrs! I've got a front seat for you." '

I didn't think so!

There was an occasion when Amba and I were taken by bus to the cinema in the next town by 'Uncle Stan'; I don't know whether he had a civilian job but he always seemed to be around. At the cinema we settled in our seats, Stan between the two of us, but shortly after the lights dimmed and the film started Amba got up from her seat and walked back up the aisle – to the lavatory, I assumed. She never returned to see the film, and when the programme ended two hours or so later she was waiting for us outside the cinema. Stan asked no questions, no explanation was given, and I found it very strange indeed. I discovered the revolting truth about that day when we were back in London; Amba had decided that she was not going to be subjected to his repulsive behaviour, that she would never again be made to 'touch' him, and so had left the cinema. I wished I had had as much courage when the same thing happened to me, which it did on more than one occasion.

Despite the insistent teaching by Salvationists that we should respect the body given to us by God (no smoking or imbibing of alcohol) this was a totally despicable family who were a downright disgrace to the Salvation Army. I might have had my opinion of all Salvationists completely jaundiced had I not met and known others since that time who, thank goodness, were wholly charitable.

Then there was the male lodger, an exceedingly unattractive man with thin, greying, greasy hair who, whenever possible, got hold of Amba and tried to put his tongue in her mouth. And if there was ever any bad conduct within the household it was always the evacuees who were blamed; the feeling of injustice we had was intense. One hot summer day the horrible male lodger invited me, along with Rose and a couple of other girls, to take a walk with him. We went to a well-known local beauty spot and the lodger suggested that, as it was such a warm day, we might remove our shirts and vests and he took charge of the discarded clothing. Although one can only, in hindsight, suspect that the lodger's motives were not as healthy as they might have been, this wasn't really such a dreadful thing to do considering our ages; we were all young and prepubescent and no indecency was involved. In fact we all felt very free about walking together half-dressed and feeling cool; it was a new experience and as it was a trusted grown-up in charge of us we assumed there was nothing untoward in our conduct. However, as luck would have it, another member of the household was also taking a walk nearby and witnessed our semi-nakedness. We were reported to Granny who accused me – *me!* – of instigating the offence. The lodger and all the others were completely blameless. It was considered that my evil 'dirty little Londoner' influence had brought about the disgraceful behaviour.

One day in a quiet moment at school, a friend and I, aged about nine or ten, were larking about in an otherwise empty classroom and started to draw pictures in our arithmetic books. How naive we were! We should have known that the books would be examined. I drew a matchstick man. Then I drew another, but this one had an extra short 'stick' between the legs. We thought this very wicked and daring and also extremely funny; we both giggled and then, urged on by my success in amusing my friend, I drew two matchstick men, one with his middle 'leg' sticking out towards the other, and wrote beside it, 'They are having a fuck.'

How did I know this? I haven't the foggiest. Somehow I had learned that fucking was when a man put his penis into a woman; children often pick up information from each other. As it happened, the sixteen-year-old evacuee who shared our billet had one day come across Gladys and one of the older male inmates having sex on the floor of the 'front' room, which was rarely used except at Christmas or when the piano was being played. It's no wonder that we became aware of things that are normally withheld from young children.

Needless to say my pornography was discovered. Again, Mum was sent for and so was the Salvation Army Captain. I was in utter disgrace; Amba didn't know what crime I'd committed and was frightened for me. A tremendous fuss was made by everyone and I was totally humiliated and felt dreadfully ashamed. No one, though, thought to question the family about how I might have acquired my indelicate knowledge or obscene vocabulary.

How the two of us ever turned out to be normal, if such we are, remains a mystery. My one consolation whilst at this billet was that I was an evacuee and not a regular fosterchild. I had a mother who loved me and who would take me back home to her as soon as the war ended. It wasn't only the physical and sexual abuse we had to endure; we were also aware of a basic, uncaring, neglect; we felt unwanted and unloved. Luckily we never became really ill, but any minor ailments were ignored by the family. There was no point in telling anyone I had a very sore throat, something I suffered from frequently, because no attention would be paid and no treatment administered, and when I developed two nasty abscesses on the lower part of my right outer thigh I was instructed to remove the pus and to dress the painful sores myself each day, something that absolutely repulsed me, that I didn't – couldn't – do well and which I found totally disgusting. Then the plasters I was given were again flesh-pink and showed up like little bright beacons for all to see on my brown legs below the hemline of my skirt. I felt like one of the lepers out of the Bible.

One day I was ordered to wear a pair of navy-blue knickers for school that were so badly tattered that the crotch had completely separated from the main part of the garment and the knickers hung from my body like a skirt. I was forced to put them on as a punishment for having 'worn them out too quickly', and apart from their being very uncomfortable, I felt utterly ashamed. That day we had physical training at school and were told to strip down to vest and pants. I tucked the torn knickers between my legs in the hope that I could hide the ragged edges from everyone, but it was impossible to hold them there as I had to perform exercises, and I still harbour the memory of the deepest humiliation caused by that incident. It was cruel.

To reach the front door of Granny's house you had to walk down a dark and narrow alleyway between her house and the neighbouring one, and the two houses were connected at the first floor, producing a roof over the alley. I can't recall what sort of job Gladys did; she seemed to be around the house most of the time but she may have worked in the local laundry along with her sister, Rose's mother, Flo. When I returned from school a few days after the furore surrounding my fall from grace I found Gladys, with her crimped auburn hair, standing outside the main door, holding in her arms the toddler of one of the many inhabitants of the house. She looked at me with a nasty little smirk on her face.

'Wherever did you learn such things?' she asked gleefully.

I couldn't believe she had asked me such a question after the way she had been so 'rude' with me. They were all such phonies in this family. I didn't reply; her hypocritical question didn't merit a reply. I pushed past her and went indoors.

Mum, on the contrary, never mentioned the brouhaha. She thought it a ridiculous to-do over nothing, she told me later. And I didn't grow up to be a Jezebel.

Nine

Wednesday 1.30

*Well dear, here is the next instalment of the journal,
continued from just before tea yesterday.*

*I did not take tea after all, but disappeared into my
cabin for a rest instead, not turning out again until the
bath steward called me at 6 o'clock. Bath, then dinner.
By this time the weather had definitely quieted down, &
kept smooth during the night, until today one wonders
at times whether we are even moving. But moving we
are all right, for we have covered the following
distances so far–*

	miles
Saturday night to noon Sunday	*151*
Noon Sunday to noon Monday	*297*
Monday–Tuesday	*340*
Tuesday–Today	*384*
	872 [sic] *miles in all*

By now Amba and I were feeling lost at sea and motionless.
Although I wouldn't have been able to recognise or describe
them at the time, my feelings, whilst living in this last billet,
were usually frustration, disenchantment and anger mingled
with deep disgust and, I regret to say, hatred, although in
fairness I must say there were some good times as well. For

instance, we were given piano lessons, which of course delighted our mother, who very likely paid for them, although we were a bit scared of our piano teacher who would bring a ruler down across our hands if he was dissatisfied with our performance. He was a somewhat gruff, middle-aged man who lived in a rather splendid house with lots of carpets and soft, upholstered chairs – what we would have described as 'posh'. We were often called on to play in concerts at the Salvation Army and, sometimes, in the Town Hall; one of our specialities was *Over the Waves* by Juventino Rosas which we played as a duet – four hands on one piano. It was an enjoyable little piece of oom-pah-pah music. We loved the religious meetings we regularly attended and which always seemed such fun. Later, as adults, when we attended church weddings or funerals our children were astonished at the way Amba and I knew all the hymns without having to read from the hymn book. 'How do you know all the words?' they would ask, wide-eyed. 'Our religious upbringing,' we would reply with a wink. The Salvationists also held May Day celebrations when we danced round a maypole, and there were lots of Sunday School outings. We enjoyed all of those activities, although it was always a disappointment never to be chosen as angels in the Christmas nativity plays. The angels were always girls, always had blonde hair and were, of course, fair-skinned. No chance for me Up There, I reckoned. There won't be any black angels in Heaven (or any male ones by that reasoning, although I'd overlooked Gabriel). Later, at school in London, a more enlightened place, I was happily surprised to be cast in Shakespearean roles when absolutely no account was taken of my colour.

I tried, whilst living with these Salvationists, to believe in God, but when I knelt to say my prayers at bedtime, I knew I was deceiving myself. One year I was to be given a tambourine as a Christmas present, although it was supposed to be kept secret from me. So I prayed to God at night, asking for the tambourine, so as to be able to convince myself, on receipt of the gift, that my prayers had been answered. I rehearsed my reaction when I found the tambourine with my other Christmas presents: 'I asked in a prayer to Jesus for a tambourine, and He listened,' I would say. When I received the instrument, which I still have, thanks to Amba having taken care of it for years, I wrote my name on it, adding, 'Jesus is a friend of mine' and embellished the inscription with curlicues. It was not so much a prayer answered as, more truthfully in my mind, a wish come true. My childhood was a bewildering time; I longed to believe that there was a special Someone who would be there to watch over me always, but I could find no faith in conventional religion. What I wanted was a Fairy Godmother in whom I could confide all my anxieties and hopes; I had more faith in fairy tales than in God, yet I hadn't made the connection that godmothers and godfathers were, of course, a part of conventional religion.

And oh, how I hated Mondays! I would return from school at lunchtime to the strong, pungent smell of cheap soap which seemed to permeate every corner of the large house. The living room would be filled with powerfully strong-smelling steam from the solid-fuelled copper in the scullery where the weekly wash was taking place. That smell became anathema to me, associated with a boring meal of cold, fatty meat and greens. And Granny's greens were a gastronomic speciality! Because she had so many mouths to feed she hunted around vainly for a large saucepan in which to cook them and came up with what she thought was the perfect solution; she bought an outsized galvanised (repeat, *galvanised*) bucket which could be filled with gritty cabbage leaves that were boiled to a perfection of sogginess. The bucket became stained with an algae-like substance which lined not only the inner surface of the bucket but also attached itself, congealed, to its seams, resisting all attempts at removal, and the slimy, over-boiled cabbage tasted as unappealing as it looked and smelled and must have been as unhygienic as it was possible to be – an environmental health inspector's nightmare! When Mum saw it she was appalled, and said so. What Mum probably never saw were the loaves of bread that Amba and I were daily despatched to retrieve from the cellar where, amongst other things, coal and vegetables were openly stored. Bread wasn't rationed until after the war and I can't understand why Granny kept so many loaves all at one time – far more than were necessary; frequently those that were brought up for use were coated with a green, furry mould which Granny would slice off before serving the remainder of the loaf to her family and other inmates. She would hold the loaf against her breast and, with the serrated blade of the breadknife facing her body, she would shear the crusts off. It looked positively suicidal. The mould did us no harm, of course, but the bread was sometimes a revolting sight and had a dry, stale taste, and let us not forget that during the war years food was not wrapped hygienically; customers took newspaper to the food shops for their purchases to be parcelled up in and loaves came straight from the counter into the shopping bag or basket, along with unwashed vegetables, fish and meat. We survived, though, and as the economy grew better after the war it seemed to me to be very luxurious to have a bar of chocolate wrapped not only in a colourful overcoat but also wearing a glamorous undergarment of silver paper.

In the last few months of our evacuation I had attended a new primary school and my best friend there was Edie; we were in the same class and spent as much time together, during the schoolday, as possible. She owned her own bicycle which she used for travelling to school; she lived nearer the school than I, and because I was usually required to carry out some chore for Granny before school, I was often late in setting off.

Sometimes Edie and I would meet just as she was starting out; she too often seemed to have left too little time to get to school by nine o'clock and she would always say she couldn't walk with me because she'd be late but she usually did, and we would run along together with her bike being pushed. Maybe it didn't occur to us, or maybe we didn't have the skill, but we never both mounted the bike and rode it together, and so we were often ticked off for our late arrival.

The two of us did some daft things together, one of which was 'making' dimples in our cheeks. Edie had brown hair with two thick plaits and a happy, smiling face, and she wished she had dimples, so, silly little things that we were, we took a thick, blunt knitting needle and pressed the point into our cheeks, imagining how we'd look. We did this fairly often and one day when Edie smiled it looked as though the treatment had worked; on her right cheek was a shallow indentation. None appeared on my cheeks, and as the months went by we realised that this slight dimple on her cheek had developed quite naturally: we needn't have resorted to cosmetic techniques.

Edie and I didn't see much of each other outside of school hours because Amba and I were required to run errands and carry out other jobs for the family. We were also often kept off school because Granny wanted us to help her in the house. This always infuriated me and one morning when I was shopping at the greengrocer's a Schools Inspector spotted me and asked why I was not at school.

I told him, 'My lady kept me away so I could help her.' I felt really glad about this, and hoped that Granny would be reported and get into trouble so that we would no longer be taken out of school. But as far as I knew, nothing happened.

I realised early on that I am not a country girl; give me the city any time. Time spent in the countryside now, especially in summer, evokes that period of evacuation as soon as I smell the animals and farms or the may blossom in the hedgerows, see the plain flowers of the stinging nettle or the stinking weeds that stand tall by trickling ditches or stagnant ponds. In the five and a half years I was incarcerated in the country I didn't even learn the names of most of the wild flowers and weeds, nor of many of the insects that hummed and buzzed invisibly. On hot days I'd walk back from school when the roads were being resurfaced and almost suffocate with the stiflingly powerful smell of fresh tarmac, like concentrated disinfectant. Whilst at Clophill I had enjoyed the daffodils and, especially, the sweet peas with their delicate colours and blooms, and although I can still find pleasure in the sight of a field of primroses or bluebells, there was something about the countryside during our evacuation that exhausted me; I found the rustic existence boring, which is, I suppose, rather sad. I can put up with it for a short period, but five and a half years was far too long for me to be strolling past fields and along lanes. I yearned to return to London and to mix in with the bustle of the busy streets; to watch and to wander; to see the variety of people and to guess what sort of lives and homes and jobs they were headed for. I had, though, all but forgotten what London was like towards the end of the war, yet I boasted to the local children of how wonderful, how modern, how exciting things were there. 'We have moving staircases in London,' I crowed, 'you just stand still on them and travel up or down without having to climb,' although I couldn't, however hard I tried, remember how moving stairs actually worked or what they looked like. I closed my eyes tight and tried to imagine them; how *did* escalators move up and down? And what happened when you reached the top or the bottom? Where did the staircase go to then? It was one of the first things I explored after I returned home.

There were no roadsigns throughout the whole of the country during the war years; this was to conceal geographical information should the enemy invade. Sometimes a convoy of soldiers being transported to another part of the country would drive through the town and on one of those occasions a soldier in the back of an open lorry that had stopped at traffic lights called down to me, 'Where are we, Sunshine?' I felt very honoured and, proud to help our soldiers, I shouted back the name of the town.

We saw quite a few soldiers – even the enemy himself! Sometimes on warm summer afternoons groups of us would go to talk to the German inmates through the wire fence of a prisoner of war camp sited on the outskirts of the town. They were all quite contented and probably relieved to be out of action, and those who could speak English welcomed our visits. I developed quite a crush on one of them, a handsome blond-haired man called Hans who could only have been about eighteen. I thought he was quite the most beautiful young man I'd ever seen. Then the Yanks arrived in town, swaggering about in their smart uniforms and the children would call to them, 'Got any gum, chum?' sometimes being rewarded with sticks of spearmint chewing gum. The Americans presented precious food parcels to the families in the town. Ours arrived and, amongst other things, it contained a jar of pineapple jam. The food was shared out at teatime and a portion of the jam was spread on to a slice of bread for everyone around the table; we had all bowed our heads before starting the meal and had murmured, 'For what we are about to receive, may the Lord make us truly thankful.' Amba's share of the pineapple jam had a large cube of pineapple in it and for this she was, indeed, truly thankful; she decided that she would eat this luscious delicacy last of all. She moved the cube of pineapple off the bread and on to the side of her plate.

And then suddenly, Granny, who was sitting close to Amba, declared quite quietly, 'I'm having that, my girl,' as she snatched up the lump of pineapple from Amba's plate and posted it through her letter box of a mouth where it was gobbled down greedily! Oh dear! *'I've got a front seat for you, Mrs!'* If St Peter was doing his job properly he wouldn't have missed that spiteful little act and would have moved that special front seat to the back or taken it away altogether! Amba could have cried in frustration and anger, but that she refused to do; Granny wouldn't get the satisfaction of seeing her upset.

Most of the time we were away in the country we were decidedly unhappy, and a day came when I stole tuppence-ha'penny – roughly one penny in today's coinage – from our fostermother's purse so that I could send a secret letter to Mummy. All letters home were read before despatch and there was always the possibility of censorship even in an 'innocent' one; as there was no such thing as pocket money I had to steal for the price of the stamp. I was determined to plead with Mummy that Amba and I be allowed to return to London.

'Please let us come home,' I wrote, in my best handwriting. 'We promise not to be afraid of the air raids.' Those were the actual words that I used and I wondered later whether I should have said that *I* promise not to be afraid of the air raids as I couldn't in all honesty speak for Amba; I wasn't even certain that I would be brave in an air raid. In reality, we did visit London with Mum on two separate days during the war and on one of those occasions I was terrified when we were caught up in an attack. We were on a bus or tram travelling down Holloway Road when the air raid warning sounded and Mummy told us to lie on the floor of the vehicle, which had come to a halt, as had the rest of the traffic. I could hear the growling sound of an engine getting louder and louder; it was a doodlebug but I thought it was a bomb dropping down on us and that soon we would be hit. Then, when the doodlebug's engine cut out after passing us and the all-clear siren went off, Mum calmly helped us to our feet and took us to see Granny

Clampitt, pointing out how the children playing in the streets didn't appear to be at all unnerved.

Back to my letter home, though. I vividly remember the moment as I pushed the three coins into the elegant bronze stamp machine outside the Post Office (I didn't dare go inside to the counter in case someone I knew saw me), stuck the blue stamp on the envelope and, with a feeling of near terror, dropped the letter into the postbox and quickly ran from the scene. I spent the next day or so petrified of the moment when I was sure the tuppence-ha'penny would be missed and I would be accused and seriously punished. Fortunately for me, the loss didn't seem to be noticed, yet I find it shocking and hard to believe, now, that I actually stole money from someone's purse. It was my one and only act of rebellion, though; I should have had more courage, especially about the sexual assaults.

We were told that Mum was coming to see us the following Sunday and I was really afraid she would mention the letter in front of the family because if that happened I would be in for a thorough clouting after she had left. I felt so guilty I hadn't even told Amba.

But the letter wasn't mentioned and neither was the subject of our returning to London. I couldn't believe it, but didn't dare bring up the matter. That awful, familiar force of despondency clutched at my stomach again. I really thought then that our mother had failed us. She hadn't, of course; she never once failed her children. She had three times gathered up the ruins of her life; she worked unstintingly while we were evacuated and afterwards; she borrowed money to make a home that we would not be ashamed of; she somehow scraped together enough cash for three white weddings; she was with each of us immediately after every one of her seven grandchildren was born, even travelling all the way from London to Carlisle in one of the harshest winters for Marjie's firstborn. She hadn't failed us over my secret letter. But I did ask her about it years later.

She explained, 'Because when I came down to see you, you appeared to be happy enough. I assumed it was a storm in a teacup that had blown over. I took you out for the day as usual, and nothing seemed to be wrong.'

'I wish you'd mentioned it, though,' I said.

I have no idea why she didn't tell me she had received the letter; perhaps she felt that the least said the better. Our mother had a natural wisdom, but she never realised how deeply unhappy we were with that family because we hid our feelings from her, protecting her as usual.

Sometimes one Salvation Army corps invited members of another to perform concerts in their hall and Amba and I were often taken to another town or village to appear in these. Apart from playing the piano we were called on to sing, too, and Amba's best friend – June, we'll call her – had a voice like a little angel. There was one hymn in particular that June sang beautifully which Amba admired; it began: 'God's in His Heaven can He see/A little child like me?' so Amba decided to emulate June the next time she was invited to sing. Unfortunately it didn't occur to Amba that, unlike her friend, she could not sing soprano, so Amba's rendition – far too high for her range – just produced a series of painful squeaks. As she stepped down from the platform at the end of her performance she was welcomed with a smart smack round the ears from Granny, who had been standing at the side of the stage waiting for her! And that came immediately after the poor girl had just asked whether God in His heaven could see a little child like her! This family who hosted us were really the most appalling hypocrites.

One of the more popular Sally Army songs of our time began: 'Ever near to bless and cheer/In the darkest hour.' Well, I never felt, in all the time we lived at this last billet, that God was ever near me to bless and cheer me in all the darkest hours I endured, and I can give two examples of the careless way in which we were treated at this fosterhome.

One day as I was returning from school I spotted Amba limping towards me and was surprised to see that she had a leg in plaster of paris. I ran to her to find out what had happened; she was just returning from the hospital after having fallen earlier, breaking her ankle. Our fostermother had seemed to regard this inconvenience as a deliberate act of misbehaviour and had not only administered a good hiding but had sent her, all on her own, to the hospital, which was in the next town, so necessitating a bus journey. Amba told me how shocked the hospital staff were to see a young child – she was perhaps ten or eleven – with a broken ankle having been sent to hospital alone and in pain. They plastered her up and treated her as they should have, but all they could then do was put her on another bus back.

The second example is when word went round the town that Freeman Hardy & Willis, the shoe shop, would be having stock for sale on the coming Wednesday. Of course everything, including clothing, was in short supply and rationed; people had to save their clothing coupons and food points as well as their money, and when items became available there was a rush to buy. On the Wednesday we were duly rounded up and took our places in the queue outside the shop. Our turn came and I was bought a pair of black lace-ups with red insets; I totally approved. It was Easter time, and I had been bought the shoes for Christmas. Now, as I was a growing child, being eight or nine years, it was no surprise to find that when Christmas arrived my feet were too large for the new, unworn, shoes. Nevertheless, I was squeezed into them, painfully, and my toes have never looked the same since; the unsightly bumps became my 'war wounds' as the scars from Amba's broken chilblains became hers (along with a few invisible mental bruises). But the shoes were not strong enough to contain me, and after a very short time both back seams burst open. I got a hiding for this punishable offence – a beating, that is, for having the temerity to grow!

Bruce Wendell knew nothing about this existence into which his selfish actions had forced us, and probably wouldn't have acknowledged it had he known. Like doomed souls we had wickedly been sold to the devil in exchange for a hopeful but vain search for professional success. But we suffered no serious illness or injury; we survived!

Ten

*The weather is definitely milder today, & the deck
sports enthusiasts are getting ready. So far I am
sticking to library books, which I find interesting &
good company. I would like to find a fellow chess-fiend,
but no luck so far. Night before last Zorina told me she
played chess; but when we sat down to it in the smoke
room, it turned out that she meant 'draughts', at which
she beat me two games, the first easily, & the second
through my mistakes, as I have not played draughts for
ages.*

Unlike our first wartime home in Clophill, our years with this
last family produced no love or tenderness and the Izzards,
who I think were truly charitable people, would have been
shocked had they been aware of how we were mistreated,
dismissed and abused. Although we enjoyed school and our
schoolfriends and schoolwork, we mostly lived for the next
visit from our darling mum and absolutely dreaded saying
goodbye to her at the end of the day. We couldn't even give
way to tears, because our foster family always boasted of how
brave we were and how we never cried when our mother went
back to London. Look how happy they are with us, they
hinted. When Mum did visit us she always took us out, bought
us lots of chocolate and cakes (she saved all her sweet
coupons for us), and made us eat everything before she took
us back, so that often we felt quite sick!

Something special sticks in my mind from one of her visits; something that gives an example of Mum's courage and of how she would fight for her children as a vixen would defend her cubs. The three of us, hand-in-hand, were running along a wide, tree-lined avenue together; in my mind's eye I can see that the road was free of traffic in contrast with today's congested streets. Mum would run forward ahead of us, still clutching our hands, then come to a halt suddenly so that the momentum would cause the two of us to hurtle forwards in front of her. We were all laughing happily, enjoying the fun and each other's company, when all at once Mum stopped playing the game and, still holding on to us, crossed the avenue towards a woman and a boy who had been pointing and sniggering at us. I had heard the woman say quietly to the boy, 'Call out "nigger" ' although I had pretended not to. To our intense discomfort Mum guided us to the pair, smiled at them and said, 'I can see that you're trying to look at my daughters, so I've brought them over so that you can see just how lovely they are up close.' She looked down at us and smiled proudly, then fixed a challenging gaze on the pair who looked startled and shamefaced. I didn't know where to put my face and Amba was just as embarrassed. Both the woman and the boy were clearly even more uncomfortable than we felt and slunk off sheepishly, but it was Mum's way of verbally slapping their wrists and humiliating them for their horridly offensive behaviour. She said later that the woman ought to be ashamed of herself; she too had heard what had been said to the boy. Although I would never have confronted them if left to myself – I'd have sidled away as quickly as possible – Mum took the right action in setting us an example of how to stand up for ourselves. What would Bruce Wendell have done in that situation? Would he just have accepted it as he had accepted having to dine alone on board ship? I think that Mum was much braver – maybe foolhardy, you might think – although of course, she had never had to suffer racism personally but just at second hand, which isn't at all the same, although undoubtedly it would be just as painful when it's a beloved child having to put up with such treatment. Furthermore, Mum could be quite haughty when she chose and there was an occasion much later when Amba and I were teenagers and we were all guests at a wedding. Another guest, a stranger, said to Mum in a surprised sort of way, 'Considering your daughters are half-caste' – that was the term she used – 'they're really quite beautiful, aren't they?' Mum turned to her and replied in a scornful tone, 'It's *because* they're of mixed parentage that they're beautiful.' Although I learned a lot from Mum about how to defend myself if looked down on on the basis of my skin colour, it took me a very long time to put that defence into place; I was well into my twenties and by that time there was far less racial prejudice anyway.

The arrangements for the financial maintenance of evacuees were that the parents paid a certain sum into their local Post Office and the host families would collect the same amount from theirs. I knew that Mum often gave our foster parents extra money, though. I longed for a bicycle so that Edie and I could perhaps go out together for rides or maybe travel together to and from school (I could ride a bike because there was one in the fosterfamily and I sometimes used it for errands). I gazed in the window of the bicycle shop every time I passed it. There was one bike in particular that I would have loved, and its price was £8. When she next came to visit, I asked Mum whether she had given Granny any extra money and she said that she had.

'How much extra did you give her,' I persisted.

The reply came: 'Eight pounds.'

Eight pounds! I looked up at Mum and said, 'That would have bought me a bike.' Such a selfish little madam I must have been!

'I know, love,' Mum replied, 'but I must pay her for looking after you.'

Mum couldn't afford to buy bicycles for us, but if she could manage to get something for us that we really wanted, she would, and for my joint Christmas and eleventh birthday (the last day of the year) I asked for a Bible with pictures in. I had very few books of my own, but we could borrow books from the public library and from the Sunday School collection. Apart from wanting the illustrated Bible to add to my small collection, I was still trying to convince myself that I was a Christian, although I can't think why. The books from the Sunday School always disappointed me because, just as I was enjoying the story, I would realise that it had a religious theme that, to my mind, spoilt the tale and I wondered why on earth the stories couldn't just be stories without the overtly, and often quite unnecessary, religious moral being forced upon the reader. It was as though we shouldn't enjoy any story for its own sake; we had to have with it the punishment of God's wrath. Anyway, Mum had to search London for my Bible, and I still have it; the inscription in her handwriting goes, 'To Ann, for her 11th birthday. Christmas 1944.'

Amba has no idea how she managed it, but she was somehow able to buy Mum a present for Mother's Day one year. It was a brooch that cost one shilling and ninepence (less than twenty pence in current coinage); as we never received pocket money, Amba can't imagine how she came by this princely sum.

I know that I had, though, received at least one gift from my father before he cleared off; all of us, Mum, Marjie, Amba and I, had a tortoise shell bangle, each with a gold initial – two 'M's and two 'A's – but I only remember seeing them when they were broken and useless. The tortoise shell of each of the four bangles had snapped in two at the initial; Mum must have kept them for sentimental reasons.

As already mentioned, Mummy was very superstitious, and told us never to wear pearls or opals which, she said, represented bitter tears, and I think she believed she had tempted providence by wearing those jewels at some time; she had certainly shed bitter tears aplenty. She had a reputation for being able to see into the future and in her younger years sometimes read the cards or tea leaves for friends; she was also said to have a talent for palmistry. She would refuse, however, to read the future of anyone she loved and she always avoided concentrating on the palms of her daughters' hands in case she accidentally saw something which would be unwelcome or worrying. In our teenage years we made light of Mum's sixth sense, but others I know had complete faith and were confident that what she had forecast had come to pass.

If there was an air raid in London during the night and you were on the streets, you were urged to knock on the door of t h e nearest house and ask to be admitted until the all-clear. Once, when Mum was returning home from visiting us in the country carrying a huge bunch of lilies given to her by our hosts, the siren sounded, but she wanted to get home so she continued on her way. An air raid warden stopped her and told her to take cover in a house nearby, but she refused, saying it was important that she get home quickly. Later she learned that the house she had been urged to enter had been bombed and all the occupants killed. Was this an example of her sixth sense?

We may not have had a daddy, but we did have a mummy – the best! And most of the time we didn't think about Bruce Wendell, although we were envious when our friends' military fathers returned on leave from service, like the day when Amba and a friend were walking together. Suddenly the friend cried, 'My daddy! My daddy!' and sprinted towards a young man in uniform. He picked her up, swung her around and they hugged each other lovingly and with laughter, and poor Amba was filled with longing.

Mum, meantime, moved into a flat with a woman friend (who had such an impressive address, I thought: Albemarle Mansions!) and it was during the war years that she and Joyce, Alfred's future wife, spent a lot of time in each other's company. Although Joyce was much younger, Mum seemed to have confided in her more than in anyone else. Mum continued with her work at the hospital and dutifully did her air-raid watches with her colleagues and probably never stopped worrying about us; her life must have been one perpetual worry. She always managed to look well-dressed and attractive whenever she visited us and we thought she was very beautiful. There had been a lovely photograph of her as a young woman, taken in profile, with her hair Marcel-waved; when it was shown to us, Mum laughed and said, 'One more wave, and I'll be overboard.' I loved her funny sayings. Uncle Bill had that photo – he seemed to have all the interesting family memorabilia including, it was rumoured, a couple of gramophone records of Bruce playing the piano. There had also been a photo of Mum sitting on a seashore, wearing a bathing costume and with a bangle on her left arm above the elbow. She had her hair 'shingled' in that picture and her face was bright with laughter. Although those photos are now lost their images remain in my memory.

Mum loved her eldest brother very much; after the war, when Bill was employed by the War Department and stationed in Germany with his wife and family, Mum often took holidays with them there and on his return to England and after Aunt Doris had died he sometimes took Mum abroad on holiday. Mum would hear no criticism of any kind about Bill and on one occasion when she and Amba were talking about him and Amba had something negative to say about him, Mum stood up, put on her coat and walked out of Amba's home in a fit of disapproval even though, as adults, we sisters and Mum rarely quarrelled. Yet Bill was essentially a selfish man. He always refused to let go of anything, even if another of us would have found a certain item of more intrinsic value than it was to him, and all the keepsakes he owned went missing at his death; he had spent his last years in a nursing home so his possessions were obviously just cleared out and, I suppose, got rid of. I have a photographic portrait of Bruce only because, after pleading with my uncle, I was allowed to borrow Bill's copy to have it duplicated by a photographer, promising faithfully to return the original to him.

Mummy had a lot of sayings; some were funny, others philosophical. She would sometimes describe someone, not unkindly, as looking 'pale and passionate', although I'm not sure I understood that one; but one of her remarks, when discussing someone who was conceited or prone to showing off, was 'they are full of their own importance'. And that, I think, sums up Bruce Wendell. He was too full of his own importance. He cannot, of course, be blamed for self-promotion; artistes of all kinds must do their damnedest, must push themselves forward. But he put himself first at the cost of his family, unlike our mother who invariably put her loved ones first and placed herself at the back of the queue.

We prayed every night that Mum wouldn't be killed by Hitler, or die under any circumstances. When a child has lost one parent, he or she lives in fear of losing the second and becoming totally orphaned. What would have happened to us then? Would we have to remain with these awful people for ever? Or, as suggested by Uncle Bill, be put into an orphanage? It was dreadful to contemplate. Evacuation was horrid; I know that Mum sent us into the country so that we were safe from the war, and parents were encouraged by the government to have their children evacuated from the cities. I have no criticism of her in that regard but the experience ensured that, in similar circumstances, I could never have sent my children away to live with strangers. But Mum was in a tight spot and our evacuation helped her to gather together enough resources to provide us with a comfortable home when we went back to her. In a way, the war was her salvation.

Marjie was also moved several times in the evacuation process, finally ending up in Northamptonshire. Mum took her home in the early years of the war because she had been badly treated and was also living in filthy conditions. She must have been about thirteen then. Amba and I didn't return home until 1945.

I knew that World War One had lasted four years and I assumed that all wars lasted for the same period. So when four years had passed since September 1939 I began to become more and more impatient and disappointed. The phrases 'When the War Ends' and 'After the War' danced about in my head all the time. When I learned that something called 'Victory in Europe' had been declared at last and that it meant the beginning of the end of the hostilities, I was overjoyed. Granny told me one morning in May 1945 not to go to school because I was to travel back to London that day! That very day! My heart soared on wings of elation and anticipation, but I wanted to say goodbye to Edie. I raced down to where she lived and reached the corner of her street just as she was setting out on her bicycle. As she cycled towards me she called out, 'I'll be late for school. I can't wait for you today, Ann.'

'I'm going home,' I shouted happily to her across the road, which was bathed in morning sunshine; that scene is still so real to me. She abruptly jumped off her saddle, planting her feet firmly on either side of her bike; she looked shocked and was completely speechless. 'But I'll write to you, Edie. We must write to each other.'

Edie just stared at me in disbelief for a moment or two; it was as though the idea of my returning to my own home had never entered her head and that she had forgotten that, unlike her, I was an evacuee. Eventually we said goodbye and I ran back to the house, overwhelmed with gladness and excitement. However, in the meantime Granny had received a telegram from Mum, which she showed me. That little bit of paper is etched on my mind; it read: 'LET ANN STAY.'

What? What sort of awful betrayal was this? How could Mum want me to stay? I could have screamed my frustration to the skies. The devastating disappointment was like a physical blow; I felt ill.

Happily for me, though, I wasn't allowed to stay. My school had arranged for all the evacuees to go home together as soon as the war in Europe was ended and VE Day had been declared on 8 May. When I learned this I hugged myself with joy. I was going home! I was leaving this family from Hell! I was going to be with my mother again! My happiness was immeasurable.

What had caused the confusion in Mum's mind, prompting her to send the telegram, was that Amba and I were now in different schools; Amba had turned eleven almost two years earlier and had been admitted to the evacuated secondary central school from our part of north London. This central school, although exclusively a boys' school in London and the brother-school of the one we would attend after the war, had evacuated all its pupils together with those of its sister-school and they were all housed and taught in one building. However, when younger evacuees from the same London area as these two schools reached the secondary stage they too – girls as well as boys – joined the evacuated school. I had been quite envious about Amba being transferred because she was surrounded at school by Londoners only; there was no one there who would cast aspersions on or insult the sometimes maligned evacuees. It had been decided that this school was not to be returned to London until Victory in Japan.

I don't know why these various arrangements were made but it was probably a question of logistics; however, on that morning in May I was in a state of ecstasy at the prospect of leaving this ghastly family for ever and ever and ever, Amen.

(The central school for girls later changed its name, and later still merged with the boys' central school. It would later enjoy such a high reputation that families would make every effort to move into the catchment area so that their children could be taught there.)

Edie and I did correspond for a short time but then lost touch. It is possibly the only period of my life from which I retain no friends. The really weird thing, though, is that Amba and I returned to that last evacuation billet once or twice for a holiday. I'm sure that this was because Mum thought we'd enjoy doing so and we didn't have the heart to oppose her. Later there was an occasion when Granny came to visit us in London. She sat beside Amba, fondling her cheek with the knuckles of her fat fingers, and said to Mum as she smiled down at Amba, 'We never had a cross word. Never a cross word, did we?'

Amba wanted to shout 'liar!' and 'hypocrite!', but what use would it have been?

If someone were to ask me what was the happiest day of my childhood I would have to reply that it was the day I went back home to London. Yet, again, I don't remember the actual journey and couldn't now say whether we were sent by train or by coach. Both outward and return journeys are completely wiped out of my mind. However, I can recall that when we got to north London we were all taken to and seated in the school hall, waiting to be collected by our relatives. One by one the mothers or aunts or grandmothers hurried in excitedly and a child would jump to his or her feet, greet the relative, say goodbye to the rest of us and leave. As would become common in later years, I seemed to wait an eternity for Mum; although we knew she could always be relied on she would sometimes find it difficult to be prompt because of the demands of her job. My hopes were sinking just a little when only two of us were left in the hall; I was sure I would be the last to be collected, although I had no doubt that she wouldn't let me down. Then my heart leapt as I saw my lovely mum rush breathlessly into the room; breathless because she had hurried from the bus. I said goodbye to the last boy – Peter, his name was – and hoped that he wouldn't have to wait too long.

Amba was away from home for practically six years; she returned to London shortly after VJ Day which was 15 August, and she, too, knows that that day was the happiest in her childhood. As the coach carrying her and her school friends approached the outskirts of London, they could see that hundreds of people lined the pavements, waving and cheering and giving them what must have been a heroes' welcome!

They were shouting, 'The children are coming home!' and Amba and her friends crowded the windows of the coach, laughing and waving in return.

It was wonderful to be with our dear mother and sister again and to be part of a proper family where we weren't afraid of saying or doing something wrong, however slight, that would bring a smart slap. There was a sort of warm comfort; I was relaxed – snug, even – in the company of my real family, my family who loved me. Amba and I thought Marjie, now seventeen, was very glamorous. She did her blonde hair in fashionable upsweeps and wore maroon and blue wedge-heeled shoes.

She suggested one day, 'Let's sing like the Andrews Sisters.'

'How?' we asked.

'Well,' she explained, 'one of us sings the melody, another

sings in a higher key and the third sings in a lower key.' None of us quite understood the theory of close harmony, but we thought we'd give it a try.

It was a disaster, and we were more interested in enjoying ourselves and each other and collapsing with laughter than in getting the songs right. But it would have been wonderful to be 'The Wendell Sisters' and to become famous. Another fantasy; I had an inexhaustible store of those! Imagine Bruce Wendell's surprise had he seen the three of us on film or television!

Uncles John and Alfred had not yet returned from war service so we all went to live at Granny Clampitt's flat with Gran and Aunt Emmy. Everyone thought that Amba and I were now very religious (we were still in the habit of praying before going to sleep) and one evening as we both knelt by our bed to say our night time prayers we became aware of a chain of four heads, one above the other, peering at us round the door: Emmy, Marjie, Mum and Granny! They were all very amused at the sight of our heads bowed reverently and our palms placed together. Gran and Aunt Emmy made a great fuss of us, but they always treated us with a certain amount of deference; to them we were different and unlike the rest of the family. They often used bad language with each other but were careful never to swear in our presence, and it was as though they looked up to us in the way they had respected and admired our father. We were very aware of that attitude, and it underlined the fact that we were 'not the same'.

Uncle Bill eventually returned from service and went back to his wife and their two sons by the sea until he was later posted, with his family, back to Germany with the War Department.

By the time the war ended I had lived just over half my life away from my mother and unfortunately the long parting had its effect on me; Mum and I were almost strangers. I loved her, but our relationship had been damaged somehow. I found it difficult and embarrassing to show my love for her, or to kiss or hug her spontaneously (or to kiss or hug anyone spontaneously, for that matter) but I managed, eventually to overcome this problem.

Eleven

*There is quite a large number of wealthy folk, evidently,
who go out to the West Indies, especially Barbados,
year by year, in quest of health. We have advertised our
tour with the Captain, & the word has gone round the
ship; so we are doing a bit of advertising, by the way.*

After receiving the letter from the Dutch ship and following
the meeting with Zorina and Larsen, Mary neither saw nor
heard from Bruce again and she died without knowing what
became of him and why he had deserted her, yet she had been
a good and faithful wife and remained true to him all her life.

In 1946 Bruce Wendell gave a recital at the Town Hall on
West 43rd Street, New York (J Ingram Fox). The war was now
ended; did he have any curiosity about his family in London?
Did he feel any guilt? I can only wonder at what might have
gone through his mind; whatever it was he certainly kept it
under wraps. I can't imagine, as a parent myself, that thoughts
of us never entered his head, but he must have been
determined to push them away.

The home we shared with Granny Clampitt was a flat in
one of three enormous blocks, collectively called Wessex
Buildings; on rainy days the tenants placed their pot plants,
mainly aspidistras, outside to get a thorough soaking and the
dull courtyards would for a short time come alive with broad-
leaved foliage. When the weather was fine the courtyards
would serve as large playgrounds for the children who lived

there. Granny's block was newer than the others, although not much more modern. In the kitchen was an iron bath standing on sturdy little claw feet; it had a wooden lid so that it could be used as a table or worktop, and there was also a gigantic iron mangle with huge wooden rollers used for pressing the water out of the sheets and other items of laundry. Granny and Aunt Emmy had a pet, a black cat, whose name shocked me: Nigger! I found this name surprisingly tasteless and objectionable; I couldn't use it, and wondered how Mummy could have allowed Granny and Aunt Em to give the cat such an insensitive name. It probably hadn't occurred to them that Amba and I might find it offensive, but we certainly did.

In one of the older blocks of the buildings had lived Granny's sister, Aunt Doll, who was married to Uncle Jack, and I remembered them from before the war; Uncle Jack had a deformed forefinger; it was bent over at the second knuckle and couldn't be straightened, something which could very easily be corrected today, I am sure. Both Aunt Doll and Uncle Jack had died before the end of the war and there were no children, but it was whispered that Aunt Doll had once had a baby who had accidentally suffocated when she and Uncle Jack were drunk; I think they were often the worse for drink and our side of the family looked down on them. 'Costermongers', we were told in hushed tones.

Gran and Aunt Doll had the similarity of sisters and both wore their hair in a style I have never seen on anyone else: the front fringe parted at the centre with the two sides of it pinned into rolls that rested just above the eyebrows. The rest of the hair was tied into a small bun at the back. Granny's hair was dark, Doll's was white, and on Granny's left cheek was a vicious scar caused by a carbuncle that had been cut out when she was about eighteen at around the time she became our grandfather's wife, so we were told. Whilst we were living with her Granny would allow Amba and me to remove the hairpins and comb her hair; it was very long, and her hands resting in her lap as she twiddled her thumbs, she would sit patiently while we arranged it over her shoulders. Although Granny was a rotund little woman, we thought she looked just like Jesus with her hair down. Nicknamed Bargie, Granny dressed in long black skirts and she repaired her slippers, if one of her toes made a hole in them, by sewing a completely new piece of fabric over the entire upper; any piece of fabric would do – cotton or wool, patterned or plain. It fascinated me to watch this operation because she never removed one layer before adding another, so that her slippers just grew fatter and fatter until she ripped off all the layers and started again. She seemed to spend most of her time sitting by the fireplace, never leaving the flat. Granny Clampitt died in her early sixties – of complications, we were told solemnly, but I never found out what sort of disease 'complications' was.

One day, shortly after our return to London, Aunt Emmy went shopping with Amba and on the bus journey home a young black woman went over to speak to them. She introduced herself to Emmy – Amba wished that she hadn't – and asked whether Amba was her daughter. Em said that Amba was her niece and, on further questioning, explained that there was a younger sister. Mass immigration had not yet begun in Britain and Amba and I still knew only two black people: ourselves.

The young woman explained that she worked for the J Arthur Rank Organization and that a film was being made that needed extras like Amba. Emmy gave her our address, and a few days later the woman called to see Mum. I was there, in the living room, when she was shown into the flat.

'We're making a film about Caesar and Cleopatra,' the woman told Mum, 'and we need children just like yours to take part in it. We will pay six guineas a day to each of your daughters if you would allow them to come to the studios to be in the film.'

Six guineas (£6.30), was the equivalent of hundreds of pounds today and was a great deal of money for people like us. At that time I doubt whether Mum was earning half that amount each week.

Her heart must have leapt! *Six guineas? Six guineas a day? For each child?*

'Would you like to take part in the film, Ann?' she asked me.

'Only if Amba will come too.'

Unfortunately, Amba was sulking in another room; Mum had earlier become cross with her about something and Amba was feeling hard done by. Mum went to ask her the same question and received a flat refusal.

And Mum, who wanted nothing for her children except that they be happy and healthy, accepted the decision despite the comparative wealth it would have brought. I doubt whether I'd have done the same in her shoes. I'd have pushed us off to the studios, telling us to do as we were told, but I think she would have done anything, as long as it wasn't immoral or illegal, to try to make up for the traumas we had suffered. I wish, though, that she had insisted on us at least visiting the studios to see whether we would have liked to take part. After all, we'd been sent off into evacuation and shunted from one home to another, and this couldn't possibly be worse than that. She probably thought we'd had enough of being pushed from pillar to post without consultation; I just hope that she didn't feel guilty about that. We certainly didn't blame her.

Later we all went to see the film, *Caesar and Cleopatra*, which starred Vivien Leigh and Claude Rains and which was, apparently, one of the biggest flops of the time, despite being the most expensive British film to date. Amba and I agreed we had made a terrible mistake. We could, we realised, have become famous film stars! Mum was highly amused at our reaction and no one seriously thought about the incident again at the time. But – I now wonder! Had we taken part, had our names been publicised, would Bruce Wendell have surfaced? I think it is possible because I have come to the conclusion that he used people; that he took but rarely gave.

Regret is a curious emotion; you can do or say something you regret but it is likely that the extent of the regret will decrease over time. However, if one regrets something *not* done or said, that regret can last for ever. One of my greatest regrets is, of course, not having tried to track down my father before he died. But also a part of me still regrets that we didn't go to the Rank Studios that time; not so much because of the possible fame and fortune, but rather because it was a missed experience and, possibly, a useful one. Not only would it have been a fascinating and valuable experience to take part in the film-making, to meet the actors and the directors and, possibly, to dress up in theatrical clothes, but it would almost certainly have had some educational value and might even have prompted a career in show business. At the age of eighteen, my older son, Graham, went off to college to study theatre sound and lighting because a few years before he had been on a school outing to the Young Vic where he had been taken behind the scenes and shown how the sound and lighting engineers worked; he'd immediately become very interested in the techniques used, prompting his application for the theatre technician's course. However, I couldn't have gone to the studios without Amba; I didn't have enough courage to go it alone.

I did dream, at that time, of getting into show business, of becoming a singer, which was rather odd considering I hated being stared at; but like many dreamy youngsters I yearned for glamour. I soaked up as many movies at the cinema as I could and I imagined myself, as an adult, with a wardrobe full of fashionable clothes like the young women in Hollywood films. Especially, for some reason, I wanted beautiful shoes and gloves. I had, for some years, decided that what I would really love to be was a singer of popular music. I knew all the latest songs by heart; I could sing each one in tune and, sometimes, mimic quite well the female singer who had popularised a particular song. I would be, I decided, the first popular female black singer in Britain. However, there was a big 'But': I had absolutely no confidence in myself. I was comfortable hiding behind others (The Wendell Sisters, perhaps?), but not when singing solo. A concert was arranged at school and my chums, for whom I had no problem performing in private, put my name forward to sing *The Coffee Song*. I rehearsed with the rest of the concert participants and I had a new red dress which Mum had had made for me, but on the day of the concert I got such stage fright that I couldn't go on. Another pupil agreed to take my place at the last minute without permission from the teachers and we (especially she) were in trouble. My dreams of becoming a pop star died although I continued to have hopes of being 'discovered' because what I needed was a good push, and the Rank Studios opportunity might have been that push. Had my father been around I might have been encouraged and coached; had he been there, a constant in my life, to guide me, I'm sure I would have been less easily intimidated. Another regret! If only I'd had more courage, more confidence in my abilities.

But my lack of self-confidence brought with it an advantage; I became a good listener. Because I felt ignorant and unworldly I listened intently to conversations between more knowledgeable people and rarely contributed with comments and opinions of my own for fear of appearing foolish. I concentrated hard on the views of others in a discussion or debate, only speaking when invited to do so, and in a one-to-one encounter I learned to listen to the other so well without interrupting that it has been said to me more than once, 'Goodness, I can't believe I told you all of that.' And because I listened, I learned a little.

Mum did everything she possibly could to make up for the years of parting. She set about introducing us to the historic London sites, the galleries and museums. I was proud to discover I was the only one of my group of friends who'd visited the Tate Gallery; we climbed up the hundreds of stairs in The Monument and learned of its history: the Great Plague and the Fire of London. We were taken to St Paul's Cathedral where we tried (although I failed) to appreciate the acoustics in the Whispering Gallery. And we all went to see the Victory Parade; we got up early on the morning of the parade and Mum managed to find an excellent vantage point in the Charing Cross Road. It was a wonderful procession and a joyful experience; we waved our little Union Jacks and cheered at Mr Churchill, General Montgomery, the Royal Family and all the servicemen and women, both British and allied, as they marched through the London streets whilst the crowds cheered and shouted until they were hoarse. The soldiers that most impressed me were the Greeks in their glamorous uniforms that looked to me like ballerinas' tutus and with huge pom-poms on their shoes. I have much admiration for our mother in the way she introduced us to some of the finer, classical things in life; for the way she gave us an interest in art and history. Many of our contemporaries, those with two parents, had no such introductions.

So, our lives resumed normality. Mum had to find somewhere else for us to live because Uncles John and Alfred were about to be demobilised from the Army. John had suffered terribly in a Japanese prisoner of war camp and a telegram arrived for Granny telling her that he had been liberated and was being sent for recuperation to Colombo in Ceylon for a short while before arriving home. The neighbours in Granny's flats hung a huge banner across the entrance on which was painted the message, 'Welcome Home Johnny'. When the time came for his arrival everyone in the family and most of the neighbours, too, went out to greet him although Amba and I stayed indoors, feeling shy. We wondered how thin he would be; we had seen the newsreels at the cinema and knew that the prisoners held by the Japanese had been starved, so we were surprised when John came into the living room looking strangely plump and very yellow, the colour of his sallow skin exaggerating the bright blue of his eyes. What had happened, of course, was that he'd been 'fattened up' in Colombo before being returned home. Poor John was very, very withdrawn. He hardly spoke for what seemed to be weeks and he suffered recurring bouts of malaria for many years, eventually dying in his early sixties.

Marjie, always our good big sister, was now employed in a cinema and helping with the family income and she often treated Amba and me with complimentary tickets to films. She started off as an usherette at the Plaza, Piccadilly, but lost that job because, against all regulations, she went out in public wearing her smart uniform. She then managed to get taken on at the Astoria, Finsbury Park, a magical-looking Art Deco building whose interior reminded me of pictures I'd seen of Ancient Egypt and where stars appeared to twinkle from the ceiling. It boasted a cinema organist who, at that time, was someone called Phil Farrell, and when he rose up on to the stage between the supporting and the main films playing his signature tune *Mood Indigo*, we couldn't help but be reminded of our missing father.

Unfortunately, at the age of eighteen Marjie contracted tuberculosis and was placed in a sanatorium for a year and a half; another cause of anxiety for Mum. There seemed at that time to be something shameful about getting TB and Amba and I were careful not to tell others what Marjie was suffering from. We had a neighbour, a Mr Jolly, whose name suited him down to the ground; he was tall and round and, well, he was jolly. One day he asked me how my sister was progressing and I said she was doing all right. But then he enquired, 'Touch of consumption, is it?' I hesitated, then lied, 'I don't know.' Mr Jolly didn't press me, aware that I didn't want to discuss Marjie's condition further. When she was better and came home from the sanatorium she had big medical phrases coming out of her mouth, one of which was 'artificial pneumothorax', which meant, she told us, an artificially collapsed lung, deliberately induced by pumping air or gas into the pleural cavity to treat tuberculosis of the lung; this was, of course, before modern drugs became available. Collapsing the lung would help it to heal, she explained, and that was the treatment Marjie had had. Every so often afterwards she had to attend the Royal Northern Hospital as an outpatient for what was called a 'refill' which, as I understood it, meant having the lung re-collapsed; sometimes I went with her to keep her company, and it was obviously just my fancy but it seemed, when she had had her refill, that her bosom had been inflated. She had a white hand-knitted sweater on which were two large bluebirds which seemed to have become so buoyant that I imagined them flying off her chest and into the sky!

There was something about Marjie that I admired and respected very much. Whenever she introduced Amba or me to one of her friends or to a new boyfriend, she would simply say, 'This is my sister.' She never explained why she looked so different from us, although I suppose she may have done so later. I was always immensely grateful for that; we were considered by Marjie to be her full sisters. This changed for a while after Marjie married. Her husband, who became rather narrow-minded in middle age, always pointedly described Amba and me as Marjie's half-sisters. It was a very explicit and deliberate classification which I didn't like; it was unnecessary. When Marjie was widowed she reverted to referring to us as her sisters.

Mum found us a new home in Lambton Road off Hornsey Road: two rooms on the first floor of a house, with shared toilet on the half-landing. The front room was our bedroom with two double beds, and the room at the back was our living room. There was a gas cooker beside a cooking range, which Mum kept in pristine condition by black-leading it until it gleamed; her house-keeping was always impeccable. A square porcelain sink, with a cold water tap, stood beside the window, a dresser covered one wall and in the centre of the room were a dining table and chairs. It was all very spartan and I believe that all the furniture except the beds came with the rooms. Then in 1947 we were rehoused by the local council and moved into a brand new flat in Dalmeny Avenue, Holloway; one day I left for school from the rooms in Lambton Road and returned from school to the new flat in Dalmeny Avenue.

We were thrilled with our new home and its long, oblong, modern kitchen. It had proper built-in blue-painted cupboards and drawers and a retractable wooden worktop was incorporated into one of the units that could be slid out and used either as a table at which to eat or as a surface on which to prepare meals. The kitchen was so large that Mum bought a red Formica-topped table (*very* up-to-date!) and four chairs with red plastic seats for our little dining area. Tucked into a corner near the window at the far end was a gas geyser that heated the water in both the kitchen and the bathroom – our very own bathroom with hot and cold running water and a lavatory in a room of its own! Wow! Before moving to this flat we had had to use the public baths once a week, something I disliked, although there was no shame involved. What a difference to the life that had been enjoyed by Bruce Wendell;

in the article entitled 'Oxford in My Time' (Georgetown *Daily Chronicle*, referred to in Chapter Seven), he relates how one night he went to London without permission and missed the last train back so had to climb over the wall to get into the college. When he got to his rooms he found that his tin bath that had been prepared by his scout was now filled with soap-suds and dirty water and that some other undergraduate had already had his morning bath for him! He had been able to enjoy what his daughters would have considered the splendour, thirty-five years earlier, of a college servant ministering to his intimate needs. Anyway, we could now jump into a hot bath whenever the mood took us and we all revelled in the luxury. We felt very proud of our modern home with its 'dream kitchen'. There were two good-sized bedrooms, each with a built-in wardrobe; Mum and Marjie shared one and Amba and I the other, and the living room was more than adequate. From time to time Mum would invest in a new piece of furniture; we had a new three-piece suite; she bought us a new modern radiogram – the sort that stacked several records at one time which were automatically dropped on to the turntable one at a time – and we were the first in the entire family to have a new nine-inch television set, encased in brown Bakelite. Everything brand new; no second-hand rubbish! Although if ever Mum spotted a lost handkerchief lying in the street, she would pick it up, take it home and boil it; no sense in buying a hanky if there's a perfectly good one going spare. I don't know how she did it; she was a marvel. Well, I do know how she did it; it all came on the 'never never', but she handled that with delicate care. Then came a bit of good luck; we won £189.15s (£189.75) from Littlewoods Pools, a considerable sum of money by our standards, and with part of it Mum bought a new red fitted carpet for the sitting room. Aunty Kitty came to visit.

'Ann,' she confided to me, 'I am pleasantly surprised at

what your mother has achieved. She has made a fine home for you all.' Then she added, 'And I can guess why she bought the red carpet. It's because she had a similar one in the home she shared with your father.'

That information put fear into my heart. Was Mum hoping that Bruce would come back now that the war was over? I was terrified that he would return; I still didn't want that.

For a woman with little income, poor prospects and no outside help, our mother did amazingly well for us. She had been promoted to Catering Officer at the hospital but still took on extra work and still remained thin and underweight; I saw her in the bath at that time and was shocked by her emaciated body. Yet to our knowledge, Mum had three marriage proposals after Bruce left, although she always laughed and dismissed them.

'No man is going to take charge of my girls,' she stated firmly. That wasn't the only reason; she still wanted only Bruce. She had no interest in looking for another husband.

Our milkman, who lived across the road from us, always came to collect payment of the weekly bill on Saturday afternoons and Mum usually sat him down in the kitchen and gave him a cup of tea whilst they chatted about this and that. One Saturday after his visit Mum was horrified to discover that the milkman had left too much change on the table; there was ten shillings (50p) more than was due. I am ashamed to say that I thought this a wonderful windfall; ten shillings would buy several meals and would go a good way to buying an item of clothing. It would even buy two or three cinema tickets. Mum was disappointed at my attitude. 'I shall go and return it to him,' she said. 'He has a wife and baby and the ten shillings will be deducted from his wages.' When I married, that milkman bought me a small wedding present; although it pleased me, I think it was more a present to Mum than to me, and her example taught me an important lesson.

Bruce Wendell at the cinema organ

Ann with her nurse after a bout of pneumonia

Mary outside the house in Finchley before Bruce left England; with her is Trixie, our dog

Marjie, Ann and Amba

*Bruce Wendell, publicity shot taken
in the 1930s*

Zorina (from The Port of Spain Gazette*)*

Koninklijke Nederlandsche Stoomboot-Maatschappij, Amsterdam

M.S. "Colombia"
Sunday Evening
Dec. 1st

My dear Mary,

Today has been a quiet one for me. Last night I turned in soon after dinner, and _____ I suppose, & before long I was fast asleep; but before falling off I could feel them weigh anchor & get going. The voyage is on the rough side so far, & this morning I decided that the horizontal position was best; so I stayed in bed, & had some breakfast brought me there. At about 2.30 I had a bath (salt-water), followed by a brisk shower (fresh-water), &

The letter, which was sixteen pages long

– dons publicly". Excellent booking. So I am striking lucky Cabin & my music looks rather a bit these days. We reach B'dos on Wednesday at 11. a. m. & Trinidad on Thursday at dawn. That only gives a couple of days on shore before kicking off. This will come back from B'dos, & we shall not see Lauren till we go back. So I'll write again from there.

Now I'll close dear, in case I don't get a chance to write again before Trinidad.

Well darling, all my tenderest love to you & the bairns & my thoughts always

With fondest Kisses, Mary darling,

from your Daddy.

'From Your Daddy'

Programme of the 1937 New York radio broadcast

1939, London evacuees at Clophill; Amba and Ann are centre front row but Marjie is absent from the photo as she had already been moved to another village

Amba (left) aged thirteen and Ann, eleven; school photos on their return to London in 1945

Marjie aged about seventeen

Ann, aged sixteen with her smart new hairstyle

Mary, circa 1945

Ann with her darling sons, Adam (left) and Graham,
probably 1968 when they were two and four;
this was a very happy time in Ann's life

Marjie, Amba and Ann in recent times

Twelve

Last night I played the piano a bit again, to the apparent interest & enjoyment of various people. After that I took a turn on the deck, & retired early. I have decided to get in as much rest as possible while I can, for I look forward with some apprehension to all the social events people may try to drag me into when I get over the other side.

Despite the scrappy, interrupted education we had received whilst evacuated, Amba and I were sent to the same selective secondary central school. Mum had the choice of sending us both to the local grammar or to the local central school. Central schools had been set up in some cities for more able pupils and, whilst they were selective, they concentrated less on a classical education and more on a commercial and practical one. They had a number of features in common with the higher grade schools; for instance, we were taught a second language and had music and drama lessons. Mum decided on the central girls' school because we would be taught, to RSA standard, shorthand, typing and book-keeping, as well as the other usual subjects. In this way, she sensibly realised, we would be in a position, on leaving school, to apply for decent jobs without further education. We were also taught domestic science, and I don't mean just cooking, but house-cleaning, washing and ironing and also needlework (the teacher who taught needlework was engaged to be married, and during classes she sat making, by hand, the most exquisite silk lingerie). These classes were not meant to train us for domestic service though; on leaving, some of the girls went on to technical college because their interests had been aroused in one or other practical skill and others transferred at age sixteen to the grammar school and later went on to higher education. The central boys' schools taught subjects such as engineering, metalwork and carpentry.

When I was thirteen Mum was asked to visit the school headmistress, and the three of us had a conference. Mum was told that I was doing so well in my studies that I could, if she and I agreed, be transferred to the local grammar school. Mum said that she wouldn't stand in my way over this but that she thought I should be the one to make the decision.

I asked if I could have time to think about it. One of my best friends, Jean, had been offered the same chance, and she and I discussed it together.

'I think I'd like to stay where I am,' Jean said. And I agreed.

It was a splendid little school and I well remember the teachers. One of them, Miss Watkinson, wore what I saw as enviably exquisite shoes. This was still an era of post-war austerity and our fashion choices were very limited. Where Miss Watkinson managed to find her gorgeous shoes – usually suede flat-heeled pumps in such bright colours, blue, red, green – I didn't know; I had never seen their like in the local shops and stores, but I had seen them being worn by the lovely ladies in American movies. She also had quite a variety of beautiful silver brooches and I resolved that when I could afford them, I'd have silver brooches too – a promise to myself that I kept, although I sometimes felt very guilty at spending money on such luxuries. Although not a pretty woman, nor particularly young I think, Miss Watkinson always used make-up and she demonstrated to us, in a train compartment whilst on the trip to Hampton Court Palace mentioned earlier, how to put on lipstick. She also gave us lessons on sex when we were about thirteen, explaining how babies came into the world and, strangely, bearing in mind the unsavoury experiences whilst I was evacuated, I couldn't make much sense of it; maybe my subconscious had blotted out the nastiness but I'm afraid the whole thing went completely over my head and I didn't understand what she was on about. When she talked about sexual intercourse and told us that a man placed his penis inside a woman I assumed that the two of them just lay there together in a plainly uncomfortable position and it all struck me as being not only rather distasteful and unhygienic, but also excruciatingly dull.

Miss Bedford, too, was a memorable teacher who was greatly respected by the pupils; she was our geography teacher and, in our final year, our form mistress too. We were all about sixteen then and Miss Bedford always treated us like the young adults we were. She had, in the geography classroom, a superb, solid globe of the world which was suspended from the ceiling by a pulley and counterbalanced by a heavy brass, cone-shaped weight. The seas were all black and the land masses white and the globe could be used like a blackboard; Miss Bedford would pull down the globe, twirl it around to the part of the world she was currently teaching and mark on it with coloured chalks whatever was the topic of the lesson; rivers, mountains, country boundaries, the tundra or prairies, etc.

One day whilst waiting for her to arrive to start the class, another of my close friends, Elizabeth, started to impersonate Miss Bedford. She pulled down the globe and mimicked her so exactly that the rest of us were reduced to hysterics. One girl keeping watch through the door warned us all that Miss Bedford was approaching so Elizabeth hastily – too hastily, alas – pushed up the globe and, to everyone's horror, the heavy, pointed weight on the pulley smashed into the Arctic Ocean making a deep, crazed wound that looked like the cracked surface of a boiled egg after it has been bashed with the back of a spoon. All in the room were stunned into silence; the last thing any of us wanted was to destroy one of Miss Bedford's most prized teaching aids. Quickly, Elizabeth hurried to her desk at the back of the classroom and we all greeted Miss Bedford in a somewhat subdued manner as she took up her place at the front, but before she could start the lesson Elizabeth bravely stood up and confessed about the accident. The rest of us watched in complete silence as Miss Bedford solemnly examined the damage to the globe, pushed it up again carefully and thanked Elizabeth for her honest admission – and she never again referred to the incident. Yet it must have been a huge disappointment for her. For our part, we all felt very, very guilty whenever we saw the damaged globe. Although it could still be used, the gash at the top was a constant reminder of an unfortunate prank.

Miss Bedford also had a large Brazil nut that had been exquisitely carved; I don't mean a single nut, but the large casing which contained all the nuts, wedge-shaped like orange segments. I've never seen such a thing before or since and I can't guess how many nuts are inside the main shell. Half of the rough outer layer had been carved off smoothly and the underlying wooden surface polished to a sheen resembling a fresh conker. Then part of that glossy layer had a Y-shaped aperture carved into it which revealed all the individual nuts inside without allowing any to escape. It was both an interesting geographical object and a work of art.

Life for me during that period was very happy. I enjoyed school, I had good friends and I was living with my mother and sisters in a bright and pleasant home, the most comfortable home I could ever remember living in so far.

From Your Daddy

We were encouraged to have French pen-pals and the idea was that we should write our letters in French, our pen-pals would write to us in English and both correspondents would correct any mistakes in their own language. It was a good system; all of the French writers were boys at the same school who knew each other as we did in England, and we were all about the same age, about fifteen. My pen-pal was Georges; it was suggested by our teachers that we describe ourselves in the first couple of letters and although I wrote that I had dark, curly hair and brown eyes, I made no mention of my skin colour. I was afraid – no, I was *ashamed* – to mention that. So over the next few months I wrote about the things I enjoyed, mentioned my family and friends and looked forward to receiving the replies from my French pal.

But then I got completely scared off! Georges wrote to say that he loved me! He wanted a photograph and wrote sweet things in rather good, but slightly broken, English. So I stopped writing immediately, never replying to his declaration of love. My fear of how he would feel about me if he saw my picture was out of all proportion; I know that now, but at the time it was akin to terror. I didn't mention his letter to anyone and later one of my class mates received a letter from her French pen-pal who said that Georges had asked him to enquire about Ann Bruce-James; why had she stopped writing? I couldn't explain; I just made up some feeble excuse about it being boring and never wrote again to poor Georges, and in a way that was a minor tragedy. I just couldn't tell him what I looked like, which was ridiculous, and neither could I confide in any of our teachers or my mother. What effect my silence had on the poor lad I'll never know, but I expect – hope – that he had more resilience than I possessed. Had I not been so touchy Georges and I could have been good friends for a long time, perhaps even meeting one day, but I assumed, completely without reason, that if he knew what I looked like or if he saw my photograph he would want nothing more to do with me and I wouldn't have known how to cope with that. I never stopped to consider that maybe something about the way I had written had made him like me; I just saw my colour as a hideous handicap because I seemed to be the only one in the whole of the world, apart from Amba, who was black, and even she wasn't as dark skinned as I was, and she had smooth hair which didn't have to be worn in ringlets. Bruce Wendell did us a great disservice by turning his back on us.

Mary Wendell, on the other hand, must have been the equivalent of the modern Wonder Woman. She could so easily have been forgiven if, at the outset of her misfortunes, she had thrown everything in the air and just walked away from them. She didn't even succumb to that ultimate luxury, The Nervous Breakdown. And she never gave up.

Whenever she arrived home from work or from shopping, Mum first of all did two things. She put on the kettle for a cup of tea (she hardly ever drank alcohol) and she switched on the radio. And sometimes, now, as I pour water into my own kettle, I find myself using the same hand movements and so am reminded of her. Even though we had school lunches, she always made sure that we had a well-balanced, cooked meal every evening, which she prepared before leaving for work when on her late shift. We would often return home and find notes in her handwriting asking one of us (usually Amba, who must have been the most reliable of the three of us) to buy sausages or chops or some other item of food, or to take or collect the bagwash, a chore I detested (Mum didn't own a washing machine until much later). Her notes might be written on anything that came to hand and one day she left, face down on the kitchen table, a school photograph of me, aged sixteen; I had been rather pleased with the photo because it had been taken just after I'd had my hair cut short. On the back of the picture was written in blue ink, 'Ann, I am cross with you. You did not write my letter I asked you to do. Please will you. Good night. Mother.' So politely written were her messages to us.

The only meal we girls ever cooked was the Sunday lunch because Mum worked until three o'clock every Sunday, Saturday being her only day off. Also, she always volunteered to work on Christmas Day. This we didn't welcome; we would have liked to wake up on Christmas morning as a complete family, but if we complained about this she always came up with the same response: her colleagues had husbands and young children; it was more important that they sometimes spend the whole of Christmas Day at home. Of course, it wasn't really a great problem to us; we were competent enough to prepare the Christmas meal for when she returned at half past three, and it was typical of Mum's kindness to others.

She worked shifts at the hospital; one week she would have duties from 6.00 a.m. to 3.00 p.m., and alternate weeks it would be 3.00 p.m. to 8.00 p.m. As children we didn't know which shift we preferred. If she had the early one, we had the pleasure of her being at home when we returned from school; on the late shift the pleasure was of her seeing us off in the morning. So the pleasure and the slight disappointment were evenly matched. Although she had a heavy workload, Mum never failed to attend school parent/teacher meetings; at prize-givings the children and parents all assembled and I often looked around anxiously in case she hadn't arrived; some parents who were far better off than we didn't ever show their faces or take an interest in their daughters' education. She was frequently a bit late or only just in time, sometimes rushing in at the last moment. I always felt pleased and happy that she had faithfully turned up as usual; I was proud of my mum. Amba and I received several prizes, Mum was pleased with our achievements and I was made a prefect and became head of my House.

We had a black cat at that time who was called Monty after the General. In the kitchen was a small electric fire – no central heating yet – and one day Mum looked down to see Monty sitting in front of the fire, which was switched off, and said, 'Look at that poor beast sitting before an empty grate!' Another of her indelible remarks.

The school often organised trips and short holidays for us, both in England and abroad. We knew that Mum couldn't afford twenty pounds for a journey to Switzerland or wherever, so Amba and I didn't even tell her about such events. We didn't feel badly about this, or left out; many of our friends were in the same situation. However, I suppose it was about this time that the Welfare State came into being, which meant that parents were entitled to Family Allowance for all their children apart from the eldest. Marjie was now grown up, so Mum qualified for Family Allowance for one child. To our astonishment she announced that she'd never taken charity in her life, and she wasn't going to start accepting it now!

'But, Mum,' Amba argued, 'you're entitled to receive it; everyone is. It's not charity.'

But Mum was very stubborn about it in the beginning and when the first payment of the Family Allowance was received, she hurriedly pushed the money into Amba's hands as though it was scalding her own. 'It's yours,' she told Amba, 'you can take it.'

So Amba went shopping; she bought herself and me a new winter coat each. Hers was bottle-green wool and mine was made of red and blue tweed; I think that was the first coat I ever remember having that was brand new, and I rejoiced in its luxury! I was also very touched by Amba's generosity. Amba left school about a year later and started working so Mum didn't have the opportunity of accepting what she called charity for very long; she missed out financially on most state benefits, never even receiving a widow's pension because she didn't know whether or not she was a widow.

I had always worn my hair in ringlets, although I would have preferred straight hair and plaits – I longed to have hair hanging like curtains; hair that 'moved'. Not possible; but the ringlets kept my curly hair tidy and in a way, I expect, they were forerunners of modern dreadlocks, although much smoother, of course. They were styled by winding a strand of wet hair around a wooden rod then carefully pulling the rod out of the tube of curled hair. The rod had been made from a length of dowelling by dear Mr Izzard at the start of the war; Mrs Izzard used it then to dress my hair after it had been washed, but I had to master the technique for myself after we left Clophill and I still used the rod and still had the ringlets until I was sixteen. I found it very tedious, though, when grown-ups commented on them; they would say, to my intense irritation (and Amba's envy, although *that* I couldn't understand – I'd much rather have had her wavy hair), 'What lovely ringlets! And how many do you have?' They would then proceed to count them and they usually totalled thirty-six. Mum had made the decision that I couldn't comb them out until I was sixteen, and just before I reached that age I told her that I had an itch behind the ears; she examined my head and announced that I had nits. I was appalled! The ignominy! Nits! Mum went at once to the chemists and bought a bar of black Derbac soap and a fine-tooth comb, and immediately set about getting rid of the pests. She succeeded with the first treatment, but I felt absolutely ashamed, even though Mum stressed that it wasn't too dreadful; that fleas liked only clean hair. Then, horror of horrors! Nitty Nora, our affectionate name for the school nurse, came in for her usual inspection the very next day. If a girl was found to be infested, she would be sent to the Cleansing Station – what a wonderful label – and would return to school with her hair smeared with some greasy-looking and smelly disinfectant. I was sure I would be exposed as being lousy. To make matters worse, when my turn came for inspection the nurse said, 'Oh, I know that your head is always clean, Ann,' and started to look in the most likely place for evidence of infestation: behind the ears.

She found nothing. Good old Mum!

Thirteen

It is marvellous how the improved weather has fetched ailing passengers out today. The ship is alive with conversation & one sees faces that had not appeared at all before. The doctor told me this morning that his list has now gone down from 75 to 19!

I hated the idea of having to leave school but of course it was inevitable. At the end of the last day I hesitated inside the school gate, delaying the moment when I would step through and no longer be a schoolgirl. How I longed to go to college! Jean – still one of my best friends to this day, even – was admitted to Pitman's College in Southampton Row and I really envied her, but by starting work I would relieve Mum's financial burdens a bit, and so at the end of the summer holidays in 1950 I started in gainful employment, proudly sporting my smart and fashionable new short hairstyle which, with expert and careful cutting, became pleasingly smooth, although it still didn't move about when I shook my head. Amba, aware of the need to help Mum financially, had left school at fifteen and was already settled in work, although she, too, would have loved to go on to higher education. She was working as a book-keeper in the head office of one of the large grocery chains (Amba was always a wizard with figures), and it was there she met her future husband.

An amusing episode occurred at about this time. One evening Mum said to Amba and me, 'Would you look in my hair and see whether you can see anything. My head itches all the time.'

Under her guidance we both examined her hair. 'Look for silvery things clinging to the hairs,' Mum instructed.

There was something there although we didn't really know what we were looking for. We tried to describe what we saw and Mum said, with some exasperation, 'Pull out a hair and show it to me!'

When we did so, she said, 'Oh my God! I've got nits!'

Amba and I thought this quite comical. Mum had taken the view, when nits had been discovered in my hair, that it wasn't such a big deal. She was appalled, however, to have them in her own hair.

She rummaged around until she found the Derbac soap and the fine-tooth comb she had bought for me and, after washing her hair thoroughly, set the two of us to exterminate her unwelcome parasites. That was just the first session, though. Every evening for about a week Mum was not satisfied until we had fine-tooth combed her hair and were sure that no nits survived. Amba and I made jokes about it: 'Fancy doing some nitting tonight?' we asked each other.

I have a small lock of Mum's brown hair, cut from her head on one of the 'nitting' sessions. It is in a small gold and glass locket on a gold chain and is very dear to me.

I find it compulsive to record how I searched for my father, a search that was to become an emotional quest. So far I have related how his absence affected our living and our personalities, but after we three sisters had married his desertion mattered less to me, so I shall skip over much of the rest of our lives except where Bruce Wendell is pertinent to the tale.

In retrospect, I think I may have been subjected to racial prejudice on at least three occasions. Because I was such an innocent I didn't look for discrimination and didn't notice when it happened, but Mum must have recognised it when I told her of the incidents, and it must have hurt her.

The first occasion was when I was summoned to my manager's office soon after starting a new secretarial job with the head office of a Northern furnishing company based in Mayfair. He invited me to sit down and offered me a cigarette so I guessed it was going to be bad news. He was a friendly and pleasant man who had interviewed and hired me, and he was plainly uncomfortable at this meeting; I realise now with hindsight that a superior, one of the managing directors, possibly, had spotted me and ordered that I be got rid of. My manager made the excuse that it had been decided that the company was overstaffed and someone had to go; since I was the last in, that someone had to be me. I was very disappointed; I had been pleased to get the job and my colleagues were friendly and fun. Also, my office overlooked Great Moulton Street and there were often well-known faces to be spotted which made life interesting: once Queen Elizabeth the Queen Mother was driven to the shop beneath my office, and on two occasions we saw Katharine Hepburn and Spencer Tracey on the opposite pavement; Spencer Tracey looked up and saw us staring out at him so he stood, legs apart and hands in trouser pockets and he just smiled up at us; it was a moment that made us all feel a bit sheepish, but thrilled nonetheless. However, it never occurred to me at the time that my dismissal was anything more than as explained to me, although I am pretty certain now that it was racially motivated.

On another occasion I was looking for some sort of furnished flat after I was married. I went along to view some rooms which seemed ideal; the woman who owned the house was very pleasant and friendly and asked me to return a couple of evenings later so that arrangements could be finalised and we parted on good terms; I thought it was a *fait accompli*. When I returned, though, she appeared uncomfortable, wouldn't admit me to the house and said that she and her husband had changed their minds and had decided to leave the rooms unlet. When I told Mum about this, she said nothing, but she must have been aware, as I was later, that the woman had described me to her husband who had vetoed the arrangements we had come to.

Then there came a time when I decided to leave my permanent job and take on temporary work; I had done temping before but thought I'd try a new agency. I phoned to ask if there were any vacancies and was asked to come along to register, but when I arrived I was told that, sorry, they had no need for new temps. I was suspicious this time and when I returned to my office related the incident to a colleague. She telephoned the agency to ask whether they were taking on any new temporary staff and the answer was in the affirmative. Then she said, 'There's just one thing: I'm coloured. Would that make any difference?' and was told that yes it would because the agency's clients would not want coloured staff.

Those were, though, the only incidents of racial prejudice that I recognised; I was probably too trusting, but as the saying goes, ignorance is bliss. Many years later, when helping out in her husband's shop, Amba was to be at the receiving end of inverted prejudice: an irate black man, recognising only an English woman he thought was being obstructive and disregarding her skin colour, shouted at her, 'You ... you ... you *white trash*, you!' Amba, stunned yet finding the incident hilarious at the same time, placed her hands on her heart, lifted her eyes to the heavens and breathed, 'All my *life* I've wanted to be called white trash!' How we all laughed when she told us this story.

After we had all married and left home, Mum would always arrange a family party for us all on the Saturday before

Christmas. She would entertain us with our husbands and growing families and sometimes Uncle Bill after Aunt Doris had died. We would spend a festive day with her, exchanging gifts and enjoying one another's company. This became a tradition which continued until she retired (although even then she couldn't stop working and took to cleaning a retired military man's home on a regular basis) and on arrival at her home we would be greeted with the aroma of the roasting turkey and all the trimmings. She always put on a fine spread with a carefully laid table decorated with Christmas crackers, and all we girls had to do was the washing up. Then, when she gave up work at the hospital she would visit one of our homes for the entire Christmas holiday, taking care not to favour one of us more than the others. Naturally she couldn't afford a car, but she came to see us frequently, using public transport if we couldn't pick her up. Nothing ever seemed to be too much trouble as far as her beloved daughters were concerned. She seemed always to stay in good spirits but this, I suppose, was the brave face she showed us and the world. We still never mentioned to outsiders that our father had gone away and not come back. Neither Amba nor I wanted him back; we continued to be ashamed of him.

I must mention, too, something that Amba always smiles at. I have no idea where they came from, but Mum had a pair of huge red drawers that she would wear at family get-togethers. Then, when the party was in full swing and everyone was having a good time, she would dance, lifting her skirts to reveal the red drawers. It was her party piece which was expected and anticipated by everyone present. Amba still has 'Mary's Red Drawers'.

I'm sure one of Mum's most fervent hopes were that she would get us all safely down the aisle without us 'being in trouble', although she never voiced such a hope, at least not to me. One of my school friends had become pregnant at the age of seventeen and had 'had to get married'. Mum knew this friend very well and liked her a lot, so encouraged her to bring her babies to see us (the girl had a second child a year after the first), and told her what a splendid little mother she was, but I think she was relieved that her daughters didn't get in the family way, as she put it. She even once told me to 'stay away from having children if you can because they are a lot of work, worry and expense'. Well, she should know, of course, but nevertheless she adored her seven grandchildren with a passion. And when each grandchild arrived she would turn up at the home of the new arrival and stay for a week to get the mother used to her busy life and new routine. She advised me on several important things: never come home to unmade beds (with the sheets tucked into hospital corners); never come home to unwashed dishes (which should always be stacked away); never come home in winter to a grate that had not been cleaned out and laid ready for the next fire; always put things back where they belong before the house becomes untidy. She also guided me into making sure my babies were fed at regular intervals and, after the midday feed to put the baby to rest before preparing the evening meal so that later all that needed to be done would be to pop the food into the oven or on the stove; then, after preparing the meal to take half-an-hour's rest myself. This was all sound advice and proof of what a competent mother she herself was.

Marjie was the first bride; in 1952 she married George Plain, who was a regular in the Fleet Air Arm, and they were posted first to Carlisle and then to Northern Ireland. On completion of his service George became an engineer with British Airways at Heathrow and he and Marjie settled, with their family of two sons and a daughter, in Hatfield. In 1953, at the age of nineteen, I married Bob Franklin who was an apprentice engineer; Bob was at that time doing his deferred National Service with the Royal Air Force and he, too, was very young at only twenty-one. He was my golden boy with his light yellow hair and eyes the colour of one of his favourite flowers, forget-me-not, framed by long, almost-white lashes. He was tall and lean and strong with slender hands and long fingers whose nails were always immaculately cleaned after he had been working on a greasy motor. Careful about his appearance, he always looked well turned out; he was what was known in those days as 'a sharp dresser'. I adored him. Almost unbelievably, for the first time in my life I had the true love of a special man, someone whose love I could return.

1955 saw Amba and Alf Dalton married, and after living for a short time in Lambeth, Alf purchased his own retail business and they bought a house in West Wickham, Kent, where they lived for most of their married life with their two children, a boy and a girl. Each of us walked down the aisle on the arm of Uncle Bill, who played the role that should have been Bruce Wendell's, the one to give each of us away, and we all married in the same church. Deep down I thought that to use a church for the sake of a white wedding was hypocritical, so again I tried to come to terms with a loving God. I attended the services at the church for several weeks before and after the wedding; I really tried to believe, but it was useless and I recognised later that this attempt at embracing religion was merely my excuse to myself for wanting the white church wedding. So afterwards I turned away from the Church again, and when our two sons, Graham and Adam, were born we didn't have them christened, much to Mum's dismay. She told Amba that we were not going to christen our children and shook her head sadly. 'It's all this intelligence nonsense,' she declared, although what on earth she meant by that I can't imagine.

One short but interesting digression here: a strange and rather sad event happened on Amba's wedding day on 9 July

1955. Before the wedding service Alf, one of the most generous people I've ever known, and his best man went into the public house at the end of the road where the ceremony was to take place. The pub, called The Holloway Castle, was situated across the road from Holloway Gaol, which, at that time, looked like a castle, and the pub is still there. Typically, Alf invited everyone in the pub to share a drink with him because, as he said, he only intended to marry once, and a little later, a melancholy-looking man entered the pub carrying a large bouquet of flowers. Alf offered him a drink, and when the two of them got into conversation the stranger explained that he was visiting, for the last time, his friend in Holloway Gaol who was to be hanged on the following Wednesday. The man was Desmond Cussen and his friend or – more accurately – his one-time lover, Ruth Ellis, was the last woman ever to be hanged in Britain.

I loved the idea of being married. I still lived a life of fantasy and looked forward to having my own little home and furnishing it. I imagined buying a small house, possibly in Hampstead or Highgate (some hope!), and when I had stopped going out to work, which I fully expected to be the case, I would walk to the front gate with my husband and kiss him goodbye as he set off for the bus to his place of work. I don't think I really grew up until I was in my thirties. There was another reason, too, why I was keen to get married at such a young age; I had always felt very uncomfortable because there were so many surnames in our little family. Marjie had Mum's maiden surname, Amba and I had our father's surname and Mum was always called by the name Wendell because that was Bruce's stage name. The name Mary Wendell was how everyone, including her family, knew her. There had been a time when Amba and I were known as 'little Ann and Amba Wendell', but we were registered at school under the name

Bruce-James and that was what prevailed. I felt that when we three sisters were married with 'legitimate' different names, things would be less difficult to explain.

After completing his National Service, Bob, now an engineer working for a large motor components company, spent several weeks twice a year in their subsidiary outlets in the West Indies and Latin America, and when I started to take an interest in my father I had hoped that he might be able to help me with a bit of searching when next he visited the Caribbean. However, he seemed unwilling to do so and didn't understand my passion for wanting to know about Bruce Wendell, whose behaviour he held in contempt. As soon as his work abroad was done, Bob wanted nothing more than to hurry back to us.

It took Bob and me a long time to find a home we could afford to buy, but eventually we settled down in a small house in Billericay, Essex. Mum would now live alone for the rest of her life. She had made sure, though, that she would not be a financial burden to her children in retirement and, apart from receiving a state pension when the time came, she received an occupational pension because she had also paid into a retirement scheme at the hospital. She had been very generous, too, buying each of us an endowment policy that would mature on our eighteenth birthdays and these turned out to be very useful indeed. She was always treating us to new items of clothing and continued to do so after we were married. She would turn up at one of our homes and present us with a new skirt and jumper or some other item saying she just happened to see it and thought it would be suitable; before I went into hospital to have my first child I was presented with two beautiful nightdresses and naturally she always turned up on a visit with gifts for our children and husbands. One day she told me that something would be delivered to me; it was to be a surprise present from her. Because I was working at that time I asked my neighbour to take the delivery and to put whatever it was in my house. On my return home that evening, my neighbour called in. 'I didn't think you'd want your mother's present inside the house,' she explained. 'I had it delivered into the garden.' It was a beautiful rustic garden bench! Marjie, Amba and I received our first garden seats and loungers from Mum. We had to be very careful when out shopping with her that we didn't admire something aloud otherwise she would insist on buying it for us and she did everything possible to make up for our deprived early lives, even when it was no longer necessary.

In 1975 the company where Bob was employed relocated away from London, which resulted in us moving to Oxford. We hadn't started our family until we'd been married eleven years and our sons were now eleven and eight so that now and again I was able to take on temporary, part-time secretarial work. My very first assignment turned out to be at Keble College! That college asked the agency for me several times afterwards whenever they needed a temporary secretary and later offered me the full-time job as Bursary Secretary, but by that time I had moved on to a more permanent, part-time position at Nuffield College. However, whilst at Keble I had the opportunity of looking up Bruce's handwritten records and, strangely, I felt a sort of excitement to be involved with his *almer mater*.

Fourteen

*What a difference in one day! The sea as I look out
from the writing room, is almost motionless, & those
huge white-toothed rollers that kept us company till
yesterday are almost forgotten. Some time this evening
we shall pass by the Canary Islands & then we strike
straight across, I understand, for the West Indies.*

1974: Mum and I are in her bedroom looking through some
drawers when Bruce's letter comes to my attention and,
fascinated to have in my hands a document written by my
enigmatic father, I read the letter through several times. I can
hardly believe that for so many years the letter has existed,
unseen by anyone except Mum; perhaps she has decided that
the time is right for us to read it. Excitement comes over me;
I ask if I can make a copy and Mum says I can keep the
original. I ask her if she would mind if I try to discover what
had happened to Bruce. Surprisingly, she says she doesn't,
although I am anxious not to present her eventually with
further disappointment and heartache.

I thought about Bruce's letter a lot during the following days,
and started to become obsessed by it, an obsession that was to
last for years. Zorina and Larsen, names which had always
seemed so questionable and fictitious, were included in his
writing. Here was evidence that Mum had not been fantasising
when she'd told us about her life with Bruce. I owed her a

mental apology and I even started to feel differently towards my father, although I knew that if I found him I wouldn't know how to handle the matter. I decided to cross that bridge when I came to it. I asked Bob what he thought and whether he had any ideas about how to start my search and felt a bit rejected when he replied, 'I don't know why you're bothering yourself about your father. It's your mother you should worry about.'

Fair enough. He had always known both his parents; his family had been 'normal'; his parents, his sister and he all had the same surname. He didn't understand why I *needed* to find out about my background. Strangely, though, his comment made me feel guilty; perhaps I shouldn't be bothering myself about my father, but I'd had a glimpse of him now, and I wanted to see more.

In January 1975 I wrote to the *Trinidad Express* newspaper, because in his letter Bruce had stated that he would stop off at Trinidad. Because I was sure that Bob would not want to have anything to do with my search, I asked the editor not to use my married name; I didn't want Bob to be embarrassed if colleagues in Trinidad recognised him through me. My intention had been to place an advertisement asking whether any readers remembered my father, but the editor of the *Express* suggested running an article and on 10 February the paper featured a story with the headline 'Maybe you can find this missing dad', a copy of which he sent to me; in the article my married name was withheld. I was then mightily excited to receive, a couple of days later, a telegram from Trinidad which stated: 'READ EXPRESS RE. BRUCE WENDELL. LETTER FOLLOWS. NO FINANCIAL OBLIGATION. HIS FRIEND. AUSTIN M NOLTË'.

As can be imagined, my heart leapt, not just with disbelief and excitement but also with a certain amount of fear at what I would discover. When I had written to the paper I had absolutely no expectation or hope of anyone reading the article having any knowledge of Bruce Wendell; I was astounded. Part of me had still not been able to take on board the fact that Bruce Wendell had existed, that he had been my father, that he had gone off on a music tour never to return. It was time for me to start accepting that he had not been a character from a fantasy; he had been real and others, apart from my mother, had known him.

I had already mentioned to my son, Graham, my intention to search for Bruce Wendell, and had told him about the story in the *Trinidad Express*. I had asked him not to mention it to his father because of my fear that Bob would disapprove. Just at the time the telegram was delivered I had popped up to the railway station by car to collect Bob from his train journey from London and was out of the house for just a few minutes. I was in the habit of picking Bob up from the station because by then he was, sadly, chronically ill and the fifteen-minute walk home had become too tiring for him. Graham accepted the telegram, saw that it had to do with Bruce Wendell and, because he was unsure of how to handle the matter, took it to our next-door neighbour and friend and asked her advice; she already knew about my intention to try to seek out my father. She read the telegram and said to Graham, 'Put it somewhere safe, and show it to your mother when you are alone with her.'

Graham was aged ten and he was a charming, bespectacled little chap who acted in a very serious and grown-up way. He got me on my own and showed me the telegram, but I couldn't keep it from Bob, who turned out not to be disapproving as I had feared. He didn't discourage me from the search and for that I was relieved and very grateful, because the last thing I wanted was to do something that I had to keep secret from my husband.

The promised letter arrived shortly after and my correspondent, a retired freelance journalist, was able to give me more detailed information than I could have hoped for. It read:

> ... *I wish to state that Bruce Wendell came to Trinidad ... along with one Larsen and Madam Zorina and gave a music recital at the Empire Theatre then situated at St Vincent Street. Where they stayed I do not know. Shortly after their first and only recital, they parted company. Larsen and Zorina left the Colony and left Bruce behind. He was brought to the Boarding house where I then lived. He told me he was stranded and with little money. He did not explain nor did I enquire why. I promised to introduce him to a few persons whom I thought would be able to assist him. ... During his short stay, approximately eight weeks, in Trinidad, he made the acquaintance of one Madam Austin who returned to Trinidad from America where she had previously migrated and opened a hairdressing salon ... He told me of the relationship and it would appear to me, at least it appeared to me then, that it was his first intimate contact with a woman of colour – that is a black woman. He seemed to have been over fascinated, and he told me one day to my surprise that he was leaving for America with this person but he would most likely touch Antigua and Martinique before America. He left. When I did not know until I missed him. I next heard from him from America, not by letter, but by the enclosed concert programme with a footnote. I honoured his request by having it published in the Port of Spain Gazette ... I sent the clipping on to him with a covering letter. I got no reply. You will observe I have sent you the envelope in which the programme came. It is the only means of letting you know to whom it was sent. For a man of his culture and education his conduct is remarkedly* [sic] *strange. After*

not hearing from him I did not pursue the matter further,
he being just a casual acquaintance. Despite the size of
America, you may be fortunate enough to pick up a trail.
You see he opened his concert programme in Trinidad
with the Dead March in Saul, a piece of music dear to my
heart, and a very unusual piece of music to open a
concert programme with, especially in a country like
Trinidad. Somebody might remember him in America for
some other oddity.

Sincerely, Austin M Noltë

'*For some other oddity*'! From what I have now learned it
seems that the whole of Bruce Wendell's life was odd.
However, on receipt of Austin Noltë's letter, I couldn't believe
my good luck! For thirty-seven years he had preserved the
concert programme, in its original envelope, so that a second
archive had been handed to me. This search was starting to
become of real interest; I was hooked.

Amba didn't like it, though. She didn't want me to find our
father. She had horrible fears that he would knock on her door
one day and she hoped I would fail to find him; she still hated
him.

The programme Mr Noltë sent was of a recital Bruce was
to give at the Town Hall on West 43rd Street on Sunday,
April 18 at 3 o'clock. The programme had a handwritten
footnote: Bruce had underlined the words 'NBC Artists
Service', and had written: 'The finest Impresarios in America.
Managers of Paderewski, Rachmaninoff etc.'

The envelope was postmarked 1937, over a year after
Bruce had left Trinidad. On the reverse of the concert
programme was the following information in Bruce's
handwriting: 'Broadcasting from W.J.2 2.45–3 p.m. N. York

Time. Thursday April 15. Please notify press.' (There was no salutation, no thank you, no signature.) Then:

> **Bruce Wendell** *pianist who is making his first New York appearance, is a native of Antigua, British West Indies, where his father was headmaster of the Mico Model School. Later in British Guiana, Wendell won the open scholarship in classics, which enabled him to attend Keble College Oxford. While at the university he won second place among all students for the Gaisford Prize awarded for Greek composition. At Oxford he was a contemporary of the then Prince of Wales, now Duke of Windsor. During the World War he fought in France with the University Corps, Royal Fusiliers. On his discharge from the army he decided to devote himself to the piano. He had at the age of fifteen been organist at Christ Church, Georgetown, British Guiana. After a period of study with Frederic Damond and Violet Clarence he made his debut as a concert pianist in London in 1926. Since then he has made London his headquarters, teaching and giving recitals throughout the British Isles. He has recently completed a tour of the Caribbean.*

(It is possible that a typographical error occurred in the above paragraph, and that Frederic Damond should have read Frederic Lamond, who was a well-known pianist at about that time.)

Noltë also enclosed, with his letter and the programme, a cutting of a review of the recital at the Town Hall entitled 'Wendell Triumphs in New York'. The cutting (it doesn't bear the name of the paper from which it was taken) quoted the *New York Herald Tribune*, and described Bruce as 'famous pianist' then went on to explain that the pianist '… is an Oxford graduate and World War veteran'.

From Your Daddy

Jeffrey Green later told me about Thomas Bruce James's Mico Model School in Antigua: the Mico Charity began its educational work in the Caribbean after slavery's abolition, but started as part of the will of Lady Mico, who bequeathed £1,000 to 'redeeme poore slaves' when she died in 1666. She meant slaves of the Algerians/north Africans, but that was suppressed and the accumulated value of the legacy was £120,000 when the charity was chartered for work mainly in the West Indies – institutions were in Jamaica and Antigua, and schools in Trinidad, Bahamas, St Lucia, Seychelles, Mauritius and Demerara (British Guiana). The trustees supervised education in St Lucia until 1891, when their seven schools were closed.

The 'open scholarship' referred to was The Guiana Scholarship, and Green referred me to Algernon Aspinall's *The British West Indies*, in which it was described: 'Higher education is provided for by a Government College in Georgetown, conducted on the lines of an English Public School. A scholarship of the value of £200 tenable at a University in England for three years is awarded annually.'

'At Oxford he was a contemporary of the then Prince of Wales, now Duke of Windsor.' Years later I read the following, an extract from the article in *The Daily Chronicle*, Georgetown, January 7 1936 entitled 'Oxford in My Time (by Bruce Wendell, in an interview)' mentioned in Chapter Two:

THE PRINCE OF WALES

There was also H.R.H. the Prince of Wales. One day, I remember well, I was out with a friend, Crowley, who had a most flaming red head of hair. In those days I wore mine in a thick bushy mop. As we were walking along, someone approached on a bicycle. "Hullo, there's the Pragga Wagga," said Crowley. It was the Prince of Wales going to

---

> play football on his college ground. He seemed immensely intrigued at the strange contrast we presented, and kept his eyes fastened on us, smiling broadly until he had passed. Another day I was running past Magdalen, the Prince of Wales's college. There was a hansom cab drawn up by the kerb, but, without noticing, I dashed up on the pavement, and just as I got near someone darted out of the college and whishked [sic] into the cab. It was the Prince. It was a near thing; half a foot either way, and one or both of us would have gone staggering back and perhaps tumbled over.

The programme that Austin Nölte sent me was invaluable because of the short history it gave. My mother had always said that Bruce Wendell had had a British university education but I had somehow understood her to mean that he went to Cambridge. As the programme gave the name of his Oxford college I contacted Keble, who told me that Bruce Wendell's father's name was Thomas and that his next of kin had been his mother, Mrs A Bruce-James (I knew from my parents' marriage certificate that his father, Thomas, was deceased). The college was not able to help with a current address, their records showing that a letter had been returned to them in January 1970 marked 'moved, not forwardable'.

I corresponded with Mr Nölte for a couple of years, but he stopped writing in 1977 when he told me he was mentally and physically tired and, in a letter, said that he was on the threshold of his eightieth year. He had sent me a newspaper cutting about bandits in Trinidad which he called 'the land of my adoption' (from one or two of his letters I understood that he may have hailed from Africa), but the covering note was a criticism, a sad and despairing one, about corruption 'from the highest rung of the ladder to the lowest' and he stated that young men 'do not take to the hills and become bandits just like that'. The newspapers, he said, reported the effect of banditry, but didn't look for its cause. He complained about unemployment, saying, 'we are blessed with oil' and 'the multinationals are bleeding the country with a violence that is worse than the sawn-off gun of the so-called guerillas'. *Plus ça change!* In his first letter to me he had stated '... come March ... I will be seventy-seven years, in perfect health. In spite of living overtime I am determined to stay in the wicket to make the century.' Well, anyway, his last missive was dated August 1977, so I suppose he may have died. I was very lucky to have found him when I did; he struck me as being a really kind and caring gentleman.

I then wrote to Queen's College in Guyana, the Government college in Georgetown that was run on the lines of an English public school where Bruce had been educated, and the headmaster sent me full details and a complete record of his school achievements. It gave his name as Lushington Wendell Bruce-James (the name on my birth certificate and on his Oxford matriculation form, a copy of which I later obtained). Queen's College is often referred to as the Eton of the West Indies, and the details I received from the headmaster showed what a high standard Bruce had achieved in Divinity, Latin, Greek, English, French, Maths and Science. It listed the grades he had obtained and stated that, having taken the Higher Senior Cambridge examination in 1910, he had won the Guiana Scholarship which gained him admission to Oxford. It may have been some earlier mention by Mum of that examination which led me to believe he had been admitted to Cambridge, rather than Oxford.

Queen's College was partially gutted by fire in 1997 and all academic records were completely destroyed.* It was fortunate that I wrote to them before the disaster.

---

* http://www.geocities.com/athens/olympus/4434/QCOSAMessage.html

But back to my investigations. What about the Salvation Army? I thought. I was well aware from my past experiences with the Salvationists that they had a missing persons bureau so I wrote to their New York address but my letter was referred back to the London International Investigation Department, who replied that they thought there was little more they could do in addition to what I had already attempted. They remarked that it seemed quite possible that my father 'had passed on in view of his considerable age'. But that wasn't the point of my asking for their help; my quest was to find out what had happened to him and how he had spent his life after leaving us all in Grays Inn Road. His probable death didn't mean I would stop searching. I looked through the New York telephone directory and found two numbers listed for Bruce Wendell. I called Amba about this.

'Are you going to phone them?' she wanted to know.

Oh no! I lacked that sort of courage. I wouldn't have known what to say if Bruce had come on the telephone to me.

So, on the same day as my letter to the Salvation Army I wrote to both the New York addresses in the telephone directory, but those two letters were never replied to and neither were they returned, leading me to believe that they had been delivered and, indeed, accepted, but I may, of course, be wrong in making that assumption. In my letters I was careful to conceal my identity and merely stated that I was interested in tracing Bruce Wendell who had been an undergraduate at Keble College; I hoped that it would be assumed by the recipient that the enquiries were to do with the University. I had earlier even telephoned a private detective who, rather sombrely, after hearing my story explained that I would probably find his fees and expenses far too high, which I would have.

But the trail seemed to be ending. All I knew now was that he had gone to New York, and that by 1970 he had disappeared. Perhaps he had died; he had been born in 1891 so that was not an unreasonable assumption. So I wrote to the Vital Records Section of the Department of Health in New York, giving as many details as I could, including his parents' names. As I couldn't state a date of death they were unable to find a death certificate.

Fifteen

*I wonder how you & the children are going on. Zorina
has been giving marvellous accounts of you & them to
people. We are of the highest aristocracy & position in
England! I had not realised that so many people were
attracted to the W[est]. I[ndies]. at this time of the
year, but we have on board, Lt General This, & Sir
George That, & Major What's-It, & so on & so forth.
Lord Help Us is not in the list, though.*

*Well, darling, that's all for now. More next time. My
thoughts are with you, and my fondest prayers & hopes
with you all. My tenderest love, as always, for you,
sweet one. Au revoir!*

I dare say that my mother probably never tried to search for
her husband for several reasons. She had very little money, of
course, and no one who could help her financially. Also I
expect that the fear of rejection was strong. On top of that she
had to concentrate all her energies and efforts on protecting
and raising her daughters; she needed to put her nose to the
grindstone. However, it does seem as though she might have
been able to contact his college and get some information in
that way. She would not have known it, but there were people
in England in the 1930s who knew where Bruce was. Had
they all been sworn to secrecy and silence?

In the spring of 1979 my darling Bob died, aged only forty-
seven; he had been diagnosed with renal failure seven years

earlier, although it was later discovered that he had first become ill – and then seemingly recovered giving us all a false sense of security – eight years before that time when we were expecting our first baby. In a way I'm glad we were unaware of that; at least we had eight carefree years before the illness really took a fatal hold. The last seven years, though, had been a stressful time for us all and the ultimate year an absolute nightmare, but as ever, Amba supported me throughout a bleak and unhappy period.

By this time Bob's employers had relocated and we were now living in Oxford. During the last long months of his illness I had started to carry out every mundane day-to-day job with my utmost ability and efficiency; nothing was too much trouble. We had only one car, which Bob used for travel to and from his office, and so I would walk to the shops and carry back heavy loads without even a silent complaint. I would try to cook tasty and nourishing meals, using only those ingredients that were safe for him to eat; I did most of the gardening and the interior house painting and decorating and I would clean the house more thoroughly than I ever had before. Because he was often very tired it was sometimes left to me to attend school meetings alone, and although I knew that Bob was better at dealing with the teachers, I summoned up all my energy and courage and did the best I was capable of so as not to let down my sons. It had always been their father who had helped with homework problems but now I had to step in, although if Bob had been admitted again to hospital, I would sometimes take their mathematical questions with me when I visited him and return with the appropriate suggestions or solutions. These were chores I felt I had to do, chores I had to do well; it was like being set tasks in a fable; somehow I felt that if I carried out my daily duties with competence and cheerfulness and without complaint I would get my reward. But from whom? Not from God, surely; I was an atheist. Yet I hoped that Someone – a Fairy Godmother, perhaps (reverting to my unhappy childhood) – would bless me; Bob would be saved and we would all live happily ever after.

But it wasn't to be. And in a way the experience reinforced my atheistic beliefs. There's no point in asking for help if God's 'will be done' and that will is that you can't possibly have your prayers answered and you can't have what you want. I would compare religion to the idea of Father Christmas; be good or you won't get a present! However, if religion (or Father Christmas) keeps people on the straight and narrow, it can't be all bad and I would be the last to try to convert people away from it; in a way I envy those who can gain comfort from the thought that one day all their trials will be rewarded with a place in Paradise with their loved ones. Conversely, though, can one sell one's soul to the Devil? No, I can't believe that, either, even though it looked as though Bruce had done so, and that he had wickedly left us high and dry.

There was a day when the hospital staff suggested that if he felt up to it Bob should dress himself and go out to get some fresh air; he was then in St Bartholomew's Hospital in London, so he took himself off to Leather Lane market, a place he knew well from when he had worked in that area some years earlier, and he strolled around the stalls. When I visited him later he gave me a record he'd bought for me in the market; it was Stevie Wonder's *You are the Sunshine of My Life*, and it gives me some joy to know that he thought that I'd brought him sunshine. Bob was not afraid of dying – he told me so – but what did cause him anxiety was having to leave us on our own, but that he could do nothing about. He even dreamed about it; a dream in which he and Graham were on the Underground, but as Bob boarded the train and before Graham could follow him into the compartment, the doors closed and they were separated. Bob, filled with distress, looked back at Graham as he was carried away from him, the lights of the train reflecting in his son's spectacles. When he related this unsettling dream to me the following day, I knew that it was a dream of death, although naturally I didn't put my thoughts into words. Bob, too, didn't believe in a life after death; he had 'technically' died three times before – three times when he had gone into cardiac arrest, each time whilst in hospital after he had been given an injection to which he was allergic – and on recovery each time had remarked, in a mischievous kind of way, that he had seen no light at the end of a tunnel, that he had had no near-death experience. 'Not destined for Heaven,' he said laughingly. He would have done anything, though, to have survived to see his sons grow to manhood, and perhaps his illness made him even more contemptuous of what he knew of my father who could have seen his children grow but who didn't mind leaving them when they were mere infants.

After I had phoned Amba with the news that Bob had died during the night she, in turn, called Mum to say she was about to visit her; Amba didn't want to tell her about Bob on the telephone and in order to distract her from asking how he was Amba told Mum that that morning the guttering had fallen off her roof – it was true – and Mum replied, 'Oh dear, that means a death!' It did seem, on many occasions, that she really did have a sixth sense; even we sceptical daughters had to admit it.

I experienced a great deal of guilt after Bob died. It had been hard work whilst he was ill, operating the dialysis machine three times a week, the constant trips to the chemist's for prescriptions, running him to and from the hospital, making sure he took all necessary medication and providing the proper diet, whilst at the same time stretching myself to be a good mother and housekeeper. Now I didn't have to worry about him any more, and although I was glad that he was at last out of his pain, an inner voice whispered to me that I'd got away with it too lightly, that I should have suffered my burdens for longer – after all, Bob had had to suffer far more. Despite the fact that it was now a relief to be able to pick any food item from the supermarket shelf without having to read the list of its ingredients, although I no longer needed to be careful about whether there were too many stairs for Bob to climb when we went visiting people and places, and whilst I could walk more quickly in the street and even run for a bus if I wanted, it all seemed wrong. I knew other renal patients who had been ill far longer than Bob had whose families had had to struggle more than I, and my conscience troubled me because it seemed I had been let off the hook too easily. I seemed to have been tired most of the last year or so of Bob's life, yet now I found myself missing even the worrying ordeal of operating the kidney machine when I had held his life in my hands for hours three times weekly. Graham, being technically inclined, had been a great help to me with that task; I don't know how things are now, but in those days the dialysis machine had to be rebuilt after use, taking quite a long time. Graham assisted me with this task so that the two of us could get to bed as soon as possible, because the dialysis was usually carried out after Bob came home from work.

I dreamed about Bob a great deal, and those dreams were so real that when I awoke I was filled with disappointment at the realisation that they were merely dreams, although I welcomed them because for a little while I had him back with us. Those dreams continued for years, and I wondered whether Mum ever dreamed about Bruce coming back to her.

Bob's was the first funeral I had ever attended. When Aunt Emily had died, in her early sixties, a couple of years before, I had not been able to attend her service because of my commitments to Bob and the children. Mum had been very,

very close to her sister and was devastated by her early death. A close family member, almost hysterical with grief, had said to Mum that it wasn't fair and why didn't older people die, and that thoughtless and rather unkind remark hurt Mum more than I can describe because she knew that the implication was that she, Mary, being older than her sister, should have died in her place. Now Bob's death was added to her sorrow.

And I became part of that new category, The Single Parent; something I didn't like very much because I was afraid that people would think I was divorced when all I had ever wanted was to show the world that I was part of a happy, loving and normal family. I had been determined that our marriage would be a conventional one, that my husband and I would love each other for ever and that when children were born we would all share the same name. I had never, until the last months of Bob's illness, foreseen that I would be left to bring up my sons on my own or that they would be deprived of a caring and loving father. Although Graham, then aged fourteen, had realised the extent of his father's illness and had been aware that he might die sooner rather than later, Adam, who was twelve, expected that things would muddle along in the way they had since he'd been five, when it had first been realised that his father was seriously ill. We were all heartbroken, not least Mum.

I found it very hard bringing up the boys without their father; in fact I found it frightening. Ordinary little decisions like, for instance, replacing the lawn mower or planning a holiday, or getting a builder to mend the roof of the shed, all loomed large and became overpowering, probably because I'd never been without Bob because we had married at such a young age; I'd never before had to make decisions alone. But Mum had had to manage alone, and so could I. She'd been totally on her own; I'd have the advantage of having her, my dependable mother, to stand by me, and I wouldn't have as many years of solitude ahead of me as she'd had. For me the loss of my father had not been a painful experience – although of course I was aware of it, albeit in the background of my life – but when Bob died the loss was like an open wound that might take years to heal. It was about this time that I first thought seriously about documenting the story of my search for my father. I had, since first reading Bruce's letter, made a few notes; now I would attempt to complete the search in earnest and to write it down, if only so that the family could read it.

From time to time new acquaintances would enquire about my background but by then I had become open and relaxed about the fact that we had been forsaken by Bruce in his search for success; I was no longer ashamed of him. And often those who heard the story suggested I should get my story published; one man I got talking to at a party even voiced the opinion that not to do so would be a disservice to the public! But though I could put together a decent letter I was no author, even though I read a lot. I'd never know, I thought, unless I gave it a try.

Sixteen

*I hope Amba & Margery are being good girls & that
you are keeping cheerful & looking forward, forgetting
the difficulties of the moment. There are some things I
want you to do. First, will you collect my post once a
week or so from Aggrey House, & send it on to me for
the present c/o ~~Queen's College~~ General Post Office,*
Georgetown
Demerara
*Also there is a dress waistcoat in the top drawer
(black); please send it to same address. I collected the
jacket & a pair of trousers. The suit will be a standby
to save the new one. Thank you dear.*

A little bit of domesticity creeping in there that I find heart-rending on behalf of my mother. Although I never questioned her about it, I have not the slightest doubt that Mum did as Bruce asked; that she collected his post; that she took the dress waistcoat from the top drawer (black), folded it neatly and sent everything on to Georgetown, Demerara. She would also have enclosed a letter, written in her curly, unique hand. Bruce's request would have cost precious money and it must have been the last contact they had with each other. Yet not a word of thanks or acknowledgement did she receive. I have wondered whether the only reason Bruce wrote the chronicle to Mary during the crossing was that he might need her for such mundane errands. Had he left without another word I think that in a way it would have been less cruel, but the long letter declaring his concern for us all merely raised Mary's hopes that all would eventually be well and there would be a successful outcome. Instead, she had to wait for weeks to fully appreciate how desperate her situation was. Spitefully, I'd like to think that the package got lost in the post and that Bruce didn't get his miserable standby waistcoat. Why should Mum have been expected to run around, doing his errands, when she was being so wickedly deceived? I can imagine her waiting daily for a reply telling her how the tour was proceeding. It must have been a frustrating, agonising time trying to keep 'cheerful and looking forward, forgetting the difficulties of the moment'; it all smacks of such appalling dishonesty! And the difficulties were going to keep mounting, not just at that moment, but through many years to come.

Our uncles and aunt must have been very discreet and loyal because not once was Bruce's desertion discussed with us by Bill, John, Emmy or Alfred. Only on questioning Alfred have I heard any word about Bruce from any of them, except that once or twice as I was growing one might remark on how tall I was getting and that I would probably 'take after' my father in that respect – something I didn't welcome. He was said to have been very tall and I didn't want to stand out any more than I already did. As it happened I stopped growing (at five feet six) at sixteen, so my fears on that score were unfounded.

I don't know how Mum managed her life during the time between Bruce leaving for the tour and when she learned he was not to return to us all, whether she stayed at home solely concentrating on looking after us or whether she had some other sort of occupation as well. I don't even know where that home was; did we remain for a time in Grays Inn Road? Although Mum had never parted with that last letter from Bruce, she hadn't kept the envelope in which it arrived. I wish that she had so that I could have known which address it went to. However she busied herself, though, the time would soon come when she'd be looking for any sort of work that would bring in some money. She often made light-hearted remarks about it in later years, saying that she thought she might have to 'go down Lisle Street', a joking reference to prostitution. Another of her wisecracks, of course; one of her most remarkable characteristics was the sense of humour she always appeared to maintain.

Of course, I may be doing Bruce a grave injustice. Up until the time of his arrival in Trinidad he may still have had every intention of returning to us after the tour, but the odds against that are high in view of the fact that he never spoke of his wife and family as far as I know, and that he never again contacted Mum. And who knows what the catalyst was? Whatever happened he should have known that Mum would stand by her man and the father of her children. If he had fallen for another woman (and earlier in this story you learned that that may have been the case) Mum would have taken him back, I think; not just because she loved him but also because she would have wanted stability for her small family. We might even conjecture loss of memory or some other dramatic event but I think we must rule that out also, because of the bearers of bad news who were, apparently, sent. I wish I knew the truth of what happened but I never will, and supposition is all I have; but what I now believe is that he shrugged off his former life as a snake will slough off an outgrown and useless skin and just left it lying there for someone else to deal with.

I think I might even have been able to love this father I never knew. I certainly liked his writing. I could have learned so much from him, surely, always supposing he were willing to teach. At least the gift of music could have been ours because he did teach that; my birth certificate describes him as Professor of Music, although this was merely titular and there was no Chair (otherwise that would have been publicised in later reports and interviews, she says cynically). Amba and I performed adequately when we did have piano lessons and Marjie could play the piano intuitively. A better education would surely have come our way, too; when Marjie was having learning difficulties Bruce sent her to a specialist school, so he would have made sure that Amba and I were allowed our full potential. It's apparent that Bruce liked to live stylishly so possibly he mismanaged money, but that's where Mum would have come in so useful. She could handle financial matters and she would have been able to do so if and when he returned to her, so long as Bruce agreed to her handling the purse-strings although, as a strong woman, she would probably have overridden any protests.

Another pity is that we would have been such a handsome family. Whenever I now see a mixed-marriage couple and their children I have a deep sense of regret that as a child I hated being the colour I was when, as a family, the five of us could have walked the streets turning heads: Mum, with her slender face and beautiful blue, deep-set eyes, was a lovely-looking woman; Bruce was handsome with, as far as I can tell from one of his photos, an amazing, almost blinding, smile; Marjie was a delightful-looking child and a very attractive young woman with a slender figure and shapely legs, as fair as Bruce was dark; and Amba and I were usually described at least as pretty and at most as beautiful. We could all have revelled in the appearance we presented to the world and, as Amba and I came to learn, most racial prejudices could and would have been overcome. Had Bruce remained or returned we would have had contact with other black people, educated and talented ones, and that would have been an invaluable experience as far as his culture was concerned. But Bruce had to go and spoil it all for us, for what appear to be selfish and egotistical reasons.

I once worked with a young woman, married with a child, who told me that she was renovating for her daughter the doll's house made for her, when she was a child, by her father. She often spoke of her childhood and of her parents and I was struck by how ideal that childhood always sounded; when I mentioned this to her she agreed and said that it was a golden time; 'pure Enid Blyton'. That name again. I felt utterly envious, but at the same time I couldn't help but be happy for her. Although it wasn't until I started to learn about my father and my history that I realised exactly how miserable my childhood had been before returning home after the war, I was always very aware that our lives were not the ideal carefree, childhood days of those we read about. I always felt that we deserved better, somehow, and now I see that instinctively I *knew* that our lives should have been easier, and certainly so should Mum's.

Obviously, had we had both parents our futures would ultimately have turned out differently; my sisters and I have all been content with our marriages and families so it's futile to speculate what might have been, but Mum's life would have been easier and it wouldn't have mattered to her if Bruce failed to become the famous concert pianist of his aspirations, as was, indeed, the case. Her sense of loyalty would have ensured her full support in whatever Bruce eventually decided to do.

Call me the eternal fantasist, if you will, but I'd love to meet a genie who could show me how differently we would have lived if Bruce had returned to us. But leave me in the present after I've seen the show, please, because apart from the misery of some of the war years and the disappointment of having to end our education earlier than we'd have wished, we've not fared too badly, I think. Our father may have been faithless and uncaring but we had a mother cut from completely different cloth.

A few years after Bob's death I met Herb Bowes, a recently-divorced American with a shock of white hair and warm brown eyes that smiled through dark-rimmed spectacles. Herb was quite unlike Bob; heavier and broader with big hands; rather large and untidy, and somewhat careless and unconcerned as far as sartorial elegance was concerned – a quality that I found amusing and to some measure endearing; and, absolutely different from Bob, he was a dyed-in-the-wool romantic, often presenting me with a bouquet of flowers, something that Bob had never done. (I had received a bouquet of roses on our first wedding anniversary whilst he was stationed in Egypt, but they were the only flowers Bob ever gave me. I have no complaints in that department; that was just how Bob was.) Herb was different. There was an occasion when I'd made too much casserole for supper for the boys and me, so when I saw Herb that evening I suggested he take home what was left for his own meal the next day. I put it into a lidded plastic container which was returned to me, a few days later, full of hand-made chocolates. Yet although the two men were so dissimilar, I think they might have liked one another had they met.

After a few months Herb suggested that we marry. It was a very difficult decision for me and I took a long time making up my mind. It had all been so easy the first time around when Bob and I had decided to marry; there had been absolutely no doubt then, but that was possibly because we were teenagers looking at the world through rose-coloured glasses who had no fear of the future. I had come to love Herb and I found it hard work being a single mother, something that made me admire my own mother even more, but to marry again seemed disloyal – physically unfaithful even – to my first love. Also, what would my sons think? I needed to consider them; they had loved their father dearly and had suffered enough. My marriage to Bob had been filled with laughter until the last stages of his illness. Bob had been far more knowledgeable than me and he had taught me so much. We'd enjoyed the same jokes and entertainment; we did crosswords together; we made fun of and teased each other. How could I successfully replace all of that?

(Again I dreamed of Bob: I was standing on a sort of bridge and he was beside me, both of us looking over the side. I said, 'Have you noticed that I'm wearing another wedding ring?' and he smiled and replied, 'Yes, but it's all right.')

Replacement, though wasn't the point. A lost loved one can't be replaced, as Mum had painfully learned, and to lose sight of that takes us along the road to disappointment and possible unhappiness. Marriage is a compromise and if we're lucky we might find a successor, for want of a better word. Also, Herb and I got on very well together; although our tastes in music were different we seemed to agree on most other things and certainly we were able to laugh together. I had been lucky enough to find another man who could love me apparently as much as Bob had done. So we set a date at the end of March 1985 for the Register Office wedding. Then came another tragedy; just a few weeks before the ceremony, our mum died suddenly.

One morning her friend Albert called in to her flat to ask whether she wanted any shopping but she was still in bed, so Albert left the flat and when he returned made a cup of tea to take in to Mum because she still hadn't got up. He was then distraught to find that she had died in the short time he'd been away. She had bought the dress she intended to wear for my wedding and our invitation was displayed in the sitting room. She was in her eightieth year. That wonderful woman had been no burden to her daughters all through her life and she'd even managed to die without giving us the worry of illness or of having to take care of her. At her funeral, only the second I was to attend, Albert was inconsolable; he died himself soon after and the vicar who conducted his funeral service said that he would have gone earlier had it not been for his friendship with Mum. Albert had asked Mum to marry him some years earlier and she had phoned me when this happened.

'How exciting, Mum,' I had said. 'Are you going to?'

'Oh, no, my dear,' came the response. 'He's seventy-three.'

At that time Mum was seventy-four, so I didn't know whether she considered him too old or too young.

Then she continued, 'In any case, dear, I couldn't be bothered with all this sex business.'

My sisters and I laughed about this when I told them. But the friendship she had with Albert had been a precious one that we welcomed.

After Albert's funeral Amba organised arrangements about the vacation of his flat and called in to see the warden of the housing association. There was a pile of folders and files on her desk and one slid to the floor. As she picked it up the Warden looked at it as though she couldn't believe her eyes and then said to Amba, 'What a remarkable coincidence! This is the file of his friend, Mrs Wendell. A lovely woman. Did you know her, by any chance?'

Amba was proud to declare that Mary Wendell was her mother; and she knew, too, that Mum would not have thought it a mere coincidence that her file had propelled itself down on to the floor just at that moment!

Herb and I proceeded with our plans and married later that month before flying to Brazil for our honeymoon. Herb had lived and worked in Brazil for five years as a young man, and I wanted to visit Latin America because it was a place Bob had also known well. My sons were now eighteen and twenty and I have to admit that I really didn't welcome the idea of changing my surname even though, conventionally, I wanted to share the same name as my husband. Herb, who knew how I felt about this, offered to change his name to match the boys' if that would make me more comfortable. I could, of course, have continued to use the name Franklin but by then I didn't have such a hang-up about it, and my boys didn't mind the change.

Uncle Bill died in 1987 and, sadly, so did Marjie's husband, George, who was struck down by leukaemia.

Seventeen

Saturday 12 noon.

*I am afraid I have missed two days, dear, but somehow
I have not felt in the mood to settle down to write.
There has been little news, except that we are getting
every moment into more delightfully tropical weather. I
have been working a lot on the Clavier, & yesterday did
an hour's rehearsal with Zorina.*

*I have found some chess opponents now & had a
game or two. People are altogether thawing more &
more, & I think the concerts will get plenty of publicity
through our fellow passengers.*

Over the years I became by turns uninterested in and bored
with my search for this missing father of mine, or else carried
along by total enthusiasm, and it was to be in 1996, twenty-
two years after I first started my enquiries, that I got in touch
with the Church of Jesus Christ of Latter Day Saints (the
Mormons) who keep extensive family records in their Family
History Library. Amazingly – I had almost given up hope of
tracking Bruce down – a record was found stating when and
where my father had died in New York, in an area called
Lincolnton.

I telephoned Amba. 'I've found our dead father,' I told her.
She was intrigued and I explained.

'I'm only sorry you didn't find him alive so that I could
give him a piece of my mind,' was her response.

We had no Internet yet so I scrutinised with a magnifying glass a New York map, but could find no trace of Lincolnton. I asked several American friends, one a New Yorker, whether they knew of Lincolnton and even telephoned the US Embassy, but to no avail. Another dead end?

In June the following year, Willie, a long-standing friend of Herb's, came to visit us from Brazil. Before returning home he was to call on his brother, Ernest Weiler, who lived in New York State, and I wondered whether Ernest might know of Lincolnton. So, when Willie was leaving us I wrote down the name and asked him to find out whether his brother could help. Two days later I received a fax message from Ernest with a map featuring Lincolnton, an area in Manhattan close to the Harlem River. I referred back to my early records and saw that the last known address of my father on record at Keble College was on this map, clearly identified. I really felt that, at last, progress was being made. I now knew that my father had probably spent his last thirty-odd years in New York.

My younger son, Adam, now a musician himself, was due to perform in New York, Boston and Philadelphia within the following two weeks and he went to the New York Vital Records Office to apply personally for the death certificate. Both of my sons had become fascinated with my quest and were as enthusiastic about it as I was; Adam hoped he would have time to find the place where his grandfather had last lived and to try and get as much information as possible in the short amount of free time at his disposal. On his return Adam reported that a computer entry had been found that looked like Bruce Wendell's, although the screen didn't show the cause of death. It did, however, reveal the day of death (the Mormon record showed only the month), and he was promised a reply within three weeks. Adam had become friendly with a young American who was a fan of his band, and the two of them went to the area in Harlem where Bruce Wendell had last lived and they located the address. They took photographs of the building and the surrounding area. They could find no one, however, who had ever heard of Bruce Wendell – but that wasn't surprising after so long. I had myself visited New York in the summer of 1990, and wished I had then had the information now in my possession. Nevertheless, I was very pleased with this latest development and awaited the death certificate; surely this time I would learn something.

On 28 July the certificate, showing cause of death as natural, but not giving specific details of the illness that caused it, arrived and revealed the following:

Certificate No 156-68-17184
Name of Deceased: Bruce Wendell;
Place of death: Manhattan Metropolitan Hospital;
Date of death: August 13, 1968;
Death due to natural causes;
Personal Particulars:
Street and house number: 2181 Madison Avenue;
Length of residence or stay in City of New York immediately prior to death: 31 years;
Single, married, widowed or divorced: Married;
Maiden name of surviving spouse: Helen Williams;
Date of birth of decedent: February 9 1891;
Age at last birthday: 77 years;
Usual occupation: Concert pianist;
Social Security No.: 052-30-6857;
Birthplace: Antigua, BWI;
Citizenship: USA;
Any other name(s) by which decedent was known: (no entry)
Name of father: Lucius Wendell;
Maiden name of mother: Ann —;
Name of informant: Helen Wendell, wife, 2181 Madison Avenue;

From Your Daddy

Name of Crematory: Ferncliff Crematory, Hartsdale, NY
Date of Cremation: August 16, 1968
Funeral director. Rodney Dade Inc., 2332 Seventh Avenue, NYC 10030

Married to someone called Helen Williams! I hadn't expected to discover that Bruce had remarried, and I was also slightly surprised to see that he had taken US citizenship, although I now realise that that was probably a prerequisite for remaining in the United States for such a long time. Most of the information on the certificate tallied, although there were two important discrepancies. There should have been an entry against 'Any other name(s)...', but perhaps Bruce Wendell's birth names had been deliberately omitted in order to avoid exposure. Also, as had probably happened with my mother, Bruce Wendell may not have revealed all of his past to his second wife. I wished, for personal, hereditary reasons, that the cause of his death had been recorded. My genetic make-up is closer to my father's than is Amba's. Several times as an adult I have been subjected to blood tests because I became anaemic, once or twice quite severely, and then when I was about forty, after attending a blood donor session which I had been in the habit of doing for about fifteen years, it was discovered that I have a sickle cell trait. Then, after further tests, it was confirmed that so have both my sons; yet as far as I know Amba doesn't, and it's always useful to know if there is a physical or mental condition in the family that one should be aware of. The second, serious error was the name of his father, which was certainly wrong; completely fictitious, even.

I mulled over this misinformation for some weeks, and then wrote to the New York Department of Health, advising them of the inaccuracies. They replied saying that if I wished to have the record corrected I must provide my father's birth certificate.

Accordingly, I wrote to Antigua where my father was born. Although I was advised that it would be with me within two weeks, it took almost another year for the birth certificate to arrive at my home. I was ultimately helped by the Antigua and Barbuda High Commission in London. They wrote more than once on my behalf to the High Court Registrar in St John's urging them to send me the certificate, but to no avail. When a member of their staff was due for leave in Antigua she suggested that she should go in person to the Registrar's Division in St John's, and it was she who brought the certificate back to London. When it did reach me it had one glaring omission; there were no given names recorded! The certificate was traced because I had correctly named my father's parents and his date of birth, but although my grandparents had registered the birth within the legally required period, they had failed to return later to add their son's name to the registration.

So it seems that as far as vital records are concerned, my father, Lushington Wendell Bruce-James, never existed! There is no birth certificate in that name, neither is there a death certificate in that name. I never had a daddy and I never had a father either – at least, not officially – and if my life depended on my being able to prove that I am the daughter of Bruce Wendell, concert pianist, a copy of whose inaccurate death certificate and a copy of whose incomplete birth certificate I now have, I think I would be feeling very troubled indeed.

I have four documents bearing my father's handwriting. One is a copy of his university matriculation form. Candidates for matriculation at Oxford are required to complete the form in their own handwriting and as Bruce was only nineteen when he went up, the handwriting on that form is quite dissimilar to that on the other three items. Those others are the last letter to my mother, the hand-addressed envelope sent from New York to Austin M Noltë in Trinidad and, inside the envelope, the note written on the concert programme. These last three documents were written when my father was well over forty and are clearly written by the same person. However, none shows a signature; the letter to my mother was signed with what must have been a pet name. My own birth certificate, though, states that my birth was registered by my father, Lushington Wendell Bruce-James, and is signed 'Wendell Bruce-James' in the same hand as that on the letter, envelope and concert programme. I know this because the registrar in the part of London where I was born was helpful enough to photocopy the signature from the original entry and send it to me. The Lushington Wendell Bruce-James on my birth certificate is, without doubt, Bruce Wendell, concert pianist, who died in New York in 1968. For the sake of loyalty to history I applied for the death certificate to be corrected, but with this I was unsuccessful. The required form was completed and, along with all the relevant documents, taken to the United States Embassy in London where I had to swear before a consul prior to the batch of papers being despatched in the Embassy bag to New York. A short time later I received a reply from the Division of Vital Records-Corrections which stated that the documentary evidence I had submitted was insufficient and did not agree with facts as alleged. The final paragraph of the reply stated: 'According to the birth certificate of Bruce Wendell, no name is recorded for him. He is listed only as male. You must submit documentation of him using the name prior to age 7. Please inform this office who Helen Wendell is.'

I have no documentation of my father's name prior to age seven. I know that he attended Mr Sharples' Schools with Eglantine Dummett but can trace no records of his time there. History will have to remain ill-informed about this particular character, more's the pity.

This quest was becoming a painful, not to mention expensive, hobby. As far as our mother knew, she had never been divorced and I had a search carried out at The Court Service Principal Registry of the Family Division, where no trace of a decree absolute in my parents' names was found. I couldn't help experiencing again a huge feeling of abandonment about the fact that Bruce had lived in New York for over thirty years with what seemed to be no regard whatsoever for the family he had discarded in London. I was convinced that he had callously deserted us all and, to add insult to injury, had gone and married another woman bigamously, or so it seemed. Our mother never knew whether he was dead or alive and she was never able to claim a widow's status, which was quite unsatisfactory. Our father had coldly forsaken us all.

Although in almost every article about him the Guiana Scholarship and the Oxford scholar are mentioned, Bruce did not do particularly well at Oxford. He was admitted to read Greats, a four-year course (at least, it is a four-year course today), and obtained only a third class grade in his Moderations examination in 1912. 'Greats' is what Oxford calls Classics. Moderations are the first part of the course and undergraduates are examined after five terms in order to qualify for the final examinations seven terms later, there being three terms a year. Having received only a third in Mods., Bruce switched to Jurisprudence and took his finals in 1914 when he was successful in only one group of the pass school. It might have been difficult to make up the first five terms of Jurisprudence, hence his failure to pass in all three groups to qualify for the degree of BA. After being *proxime accessit* for the Gaisford Prize awarded for Greek composition, his performance in the formal examinations might have come as a blow. Yet somehow I don't think so. In most articles written about or by my father, his undergraduate days and the Gaisford Prize are proudly recalled. His marriage and children are never once referred to.

So it seems to me that Bruce was proud of being the 1910 Guiana Scholar who won a place at Oxford, that he was satisfied to have been runner-up for the 1913 Gaisford Prize in Greek composition and that success in getting an Oxford degree wasn't all that important, especially in view of the fact that it was his intention to pursue a career in music. (He was actually joint second for the Gaisford Prize, although this fact is not mentioned in any of the documents I have read – apart from the *Oxford University Gazette*, of course.)

Eighteen

*My one regret, my dear one, is that you are not here to
share all this with me; but be patient a little longer, & we
will triumph yet. My thoughts are with you often in the
day, always when I lay myself down in my bunk. The time
will soon pass by & when I come back you will, Heaven
helping us, be proud of your Daddy.*

It's hard to believe that Bruce's serial letter could have been
written by a man about to desert his wife and children. If, at
the outset of his journey, Bruce had already planned to leave
his family, then the entire letter was an enormous lie; however,
I want to believe differently. Something happened, and it must
have happened on the other side of the Atlantic. I, too, regret
that Mum wasn't there 'to share all of this'; had she been I'm
sure they would have returned together. But I think the state of
affairs shows that Bruce's situation was an impecunious one;
he probably managed to scrape together just enough money
for his own passage and we now know that, when in Trinidad,
he confided in Austin M Noltë that he was 'stranded and with
little money'. Possibly the mysterious Madam Austin financed
his travel to the United States and, even more possibly, it was
she that 'happened'. Also, I can tell from what I have read
about him that Bruce was a proud man – although perhaps not
too proud to accept favours – who would have found it
demeaning and undignified to return to Mum having failed to

earn the recognition he felt due to him, knowing how much she and her family admired him. Maybe that's the reason she, and us, are never referred to; the only people outside the family who to our knowledge at that time knew about us after the concert tour that started in 1935, were Aunty Kitty, my nanny-nurse, Zorina and Larsen and 'Pops' Clare and his family. No other acquaintances of Bruce's contacted Mum or offered any help, although I later learned that some knew that Bruce had decided not to return to England and also were aware of his movements and his whereabouts. It looks as though in a contest between accepting love plus hero-worship or merely love standing alone – from his wife – love on its own came a poor second even though worship from the general public didn't stand much chance either, except from a few quarters, one of which was Rudolph Dunbar. He was the Guianese clarinettist who published an article in *The Daily Chronicle* on 22 December 1935. How Mum would have loved to have read this piece! And I believe that the fact that she didn't, the fact that Bruce didn't send her a cutting of the article which was published just weeks after he left London, proves that he had already made up his mind not to return to his family. The article is a very flattering one and I think that most people would want their loved ones to have sight of such public blandishments. It was entitled 'Bruce Wendell – as I Know Him' with the subtitle 'Your Hero and British Guiana's Illustrious Son' and it was, as we can see in hindsight, a bit over the top. I quote part of it below. The article would seem to be a promotional exercise on behalf of Bruce; an attempt to grasp the success that he longed for. Dunbar may have had true admiration for Bruce, but the description he gives of Bruce's temperament and nature don't match up to his behaviour.

At the moment when British Guiana is preparing for the Yuletide celebrations, Bruce Wendell, one of her famous sons will be en route to his native land accompanied by Madame Ekaterina Zorina, Russian Dramatic Soprano, to give a series of recitals of unusual interest. Never before has such an artistic venture on European presentation been attempted. This stands to reason that Bruce Wendell and Madame Zorina are going to make history which will be remembered at all times as a glowing and memorable phenomenon.

...Behind this magnificent enterprise is the famous impresario Hugo Larsen, a man of profound knowledge and infallible tuition in the management of great artists. Mr. Larsen has toured all over Europe and the Orient, and has presented artists such as Mark Hamburg, Pouishnoff, Madame Ekaterina Zorina, Peter Dawson, Horace Stevens, Szigeti and Prince Nikita de Mogaloff.

With such optimism the tour must have been a huge disappointment for Larsen and Zorina, as well as for Bruce. But to continue:

...Now I turn again to Mr. Bruce Wendell, who numbers among the great men from British Guiana, and whom this article is primarily the subject of discussion. The name of his family is synonymous with education and culture to which they closely adhere and follow from father to son with passionate fidelity.

Wendell was born in Antigua, one of the islands of the Lesser Antilles in the West Indies, and was taken to British Guiana quite an infant where he grew up and received his education. Still in the period of adolescence he won the Guiana Scholarship, one of the most coveted prizes in that country. This, however, provided him with a certain amount of facilities for study in England which he undertook at Keble College, Oxford. There he read classics and fitted himself by training and concentration of purpose to achieve his end. In the midst of Wendell's studies the Great War was thrown upon the world which ensured the vicissitude of a changing régime. Nevertheless his career at the University was exceptionally brilliant. He came down from Oxford a classical scholar, with the degree of B.A., which has manifested since by the lustre his intellectual gifts have shed upon everyone.

This is the only incidence I have come across (apart from the cutting sent to me by Austin M Noltë) where Bruce is wrongly reported to have received his degree or where his university career is described as exceptionally brilliant, and sad to say, his wife and daughters were not amongst those on whom the lustre of his intellectual gifts were shed.

It is a great man who can combine two diverse rôles. In Bruce Wendell we have Musician, Scholar, Concert Pianist, and Organist. Such eminent qualities must be accredited to a human encyclopedia of knowledge.

The piano is an integral part of every Guianese life as well as singing. In view of this fact, Wendell's admirable piano playing, with his commanding technical mastery would stimulate the awakening agencies of the younger element, not only in British Guiana but all over the West Indies. Music is international language – nations speak to other nations in music. For this reason the merchants of British Guiana should put their heads together and utilize the services of Wendell and Madame Zorina for commercial broadcasts. By this procedure they will improve trade in every direction and advertise the country as well.

…Bruce Wendell has invented a method for pianoforte playing in which he has written in book-form with illustrations. I have been paid the honour to review the work which deals principally with the dexterity of the fingers. It is a masterpiece of ingenuity which certainly cannot be improved upon. Some of the great masters have endorsed the method. That is probably the reason why Bruce Wendell's hands are identical to those of Josef Hoffman the greatest marvel in keyboard technique.

There was, I know, a photograph of Bruce's hands, but that has long since gone missing. It's possible that it was another acquisition of Uncle Bill's.

As an organist Bruce Wendell's playing is supremely interesting. During his stay at the Leicester Square Cinema where he held the post as premiere organist, he was the subject of considerable discussion. It is claimed that he electrified his audiences at the Leicester Square Cinema by the studied registration, the variety of stops used, and by the way in which he produced all sorts of orchestral effects. Such things can only come from a musician of incalculable value. My picture is not yet complete – for I must underline the other side of his potentialities. Adversity and disappointment by trying him high have enabled an always loveable character, and added a new range and depth to the exquisiteness of his art. With Bruce Wendell I have enjoyed a rare comradeship wherein fraternity and mental stimulus are combined. His return home would over excite public curiosity. He is a man of rare sweetness of nature who deposits an indefinable grace to life.

Adversity and disappointment certainly did try Bruce high, it is true, but 'an always loveable character' and 'a man of rare sweetness of nature'? Well, I suppose it all depends on who was on the receiving end of his love and sweetness, and as far as 'an indefinable grace to life' is concerned, our poor Mum lost out on that deposit after fewer than four short years of marriage.

> ...Guianese, West Indians and Africans in London are
> intensely interested in the prospects of Bruce Wendell's
> tour. They know that both himself and Madame Zorina will
> be overwhelmed with warm and glowing welcome.
>
> "But that is not all," exclaimed an African Barrister. He
> replied still further: "The Government of British Guiana
> should vote a yearly allowance for Bruce Wendell as a
> tribute and recognition of his achievement." In addition it
> would enable him to do research work in the field of art.
> Such a gesture would be in keeping with European custom.
> There is no reason why this should not be seen to
> regardless of how small the amount may be. The Bluthner
> Piano Company have made the first start by placing two
> concert grand pianos at the disposal of Mr. Bruce Wendell.
> They know only too well the tremendous advertising value
> a great artist like Bruce Wendell would have upon their firm.
> I sincerely hope that the Government of British Guiana
> would pave the way for such a worthy tribute. It is the
> nation's duty to an illustrious son.

So it seems that Dunbar had much respect for Bruce and for
Zorina too, but then, Bruce apparently received quite a lot of
adulation from his compatriots. Bruce was, in all probability,
unlucky; racism may well have played a part, I suppose, and,
of course, he was around in the wrong era; he would have
been better served in the 1950s or '60s possibly. I wonder
what he would have thought had he known that, at some time
in the future, his younger daughter would write a book about
him and his disappearance. Perhaps the knowledge would
have fed his ego despite the criticism I heap on him. I realise
that this memoir may appear to the reader to contain too much
bitterness and censure about Bruce Wendell even though I
have tried to see his side of the story too. I know he thought
his career was thwarted in England although we have to accept
that that may, perhaps, have been for reasons other than his
colour. After all, other black entertainers of the period were

successful, so maybe lack of talent had a hand in his fate. He could have been the victim of racial prejudice, of course he could, but he was an intelligent man who should have been fully aware that to marry a white woman in England in the 1930s meant he had to give her, and their children, as much security and protection as was possible. To run off and leave them all was not the proper course to take. And to run off and leave them all without any sort of financial support was nothing short of wicked. I can't help feeling resentful and I think that many other people who have been deserted in childhood by their fathers feel the same way, although I do realise that it may be impossible for those who can remember a father's loving embrace to understand that resentment.

Barbara Ashton listens to all music programmes on the radio. She is the sister of Uncle Alfred's wife, Joyce, and she enjoys music of all kinds. One day in May 1998 I got a phone call from Joyce who told me that Barbara had been listening to a BBC programme on the previous Monday evening (either Sheila Tracy or Humphrey Lyttleton) and heard that the singer, Elaine Delmar, was the daughter of Leslie Hutchinson and, knowing about my search for my father, she thought that I might want to get in touch with Elaine Delmar who might have some knowledge of him. I had little hope, but thought that every stone should be turned.

And so I wrote to Sheila Tracy and to Humphrey Lyttelton. They both replied to me with the same story: Elaine Delmar's father was, indeed, Leslie Hutchinson but not the cabaret singer and pianist 'Hutch' Hutchinson who was acquainted with my father but the other musician of the same era who had a similar name, Leslie 'Jiver' Hutchinson. Sheila Tracy kindly passed my letter to Elaine Delmar; Elaine Delmar passed it on to Val Wilmer, the jazz journalist who has been instrumental in revealing so many details of this story; Val Wilmer telephoned me one Sunday afternoon! Then things began moving. Val knew the name Bruce Wendell; she knew more about my father than I did; more than I believed anyone did.

I was absolutely gobsmacked, as the saying goes, and almost fell off the chair I was sitting on! 'You've heard of him?' I asked in disbelief.

And then Val proceeded to tell me everything she knew and we talked for a very long time. I was amazed and thrilled. I had no idea that anyone in England, apart from my family, had ever heard of Bruce Wendell. Val advised me to write to Howard Rye, the music historian, and to Jeffrey P Green who had written extensively on black Edwardians; both of them had information about Bruce Wendell, she said. She told me about Dennis Clare, the son of 'Pops' Clare who played in Ken Johnson's band. That Sunday afternoon was the most rewarding period so far in my search; I felt enormously excited. Later, Val gave me details of all the West Indian newspapers that featured Bruce. With her guidance I was able to read at the Newspaper Library every one of the articles cited in this story. Zorina and Larsen became at last real people in photographs, but it was very dismaying to find out that Bruce's wife and children were carefully omitted from every story.

There were friends of his who, when Bruce left London, had had word from or about him. I later learned from Val that she had seen Bruce Wendell's two New York addresses and telephone numbers in the address book of another musician whose life story she was working on.

And Jeffrey Green told me something that I found very interesting. Arthur Schomburg, the American book collector and founder of the black library, The Schomburg Library of the New York Public Library, wrote on 6 November 1936 to Amanda Aldridge, who lived in London. She was the daughter of the New York actor Ira Aldridge, and the letter said that

Bruce Wendell the pianist was 'in New York yesterday', referring to him as 'one of your good friends'. This information made me wonder whether Mum had also known Amanda Aldridge; was Amba named after her? *Amba Mary Bruce Amanda*. Mum had led me to understand that Amba was an African name. The two middle names were chosen for Amba's parents obviously, and I always assumed that the name Amanda was attached so that the initials spelled out the first name. If Mum knew Amanda Aldridge, what an opportunity she missed by not trying to contact her; the letter from Arthur Schomburg was written less than a year after Bruce's departure from London. But Amanda Aldridge might also have been a part of the conspiracy; she might also have held Bruce's secret. It's a painful and shocking realisation to know that our Mum was probably so cruelly treated.

This information about Amanda Aldridge caused me to pause and consider how I came about my own name. Ann (without an 'e') was the name of Bruce's mother, but why were Viola and Luleta chosen? I don't suppose I'll ever know.

From these various revelations I have no doubt that other of Bruce Wendell's acquaintances in England knew where he was and, of course, he had stayed in touch with Oxford until his death, although I believe that Keble College was also kept in the dark about his marriage. It paints the picture of a heartless man who must have urged his friends to keep his whereabouts quiet. Where had this man of rare sweetness of nature, as described by Rudolph Dunbar, gone?

I wrote to Elaine Delmar to thank her but before I had time to post the letter she, too, telephoned me. Amba and I were very pleased to meet Elaine later.

Jeffrey Green informed me in a letter that Bruce played the piano at the musical interludes of a meeting of the African Progress Union at the Great Eastern Hotel (Liverpool Street station) in London on 18 December 1918. In his book on

Edmund Thornton Jenkins, Green states that on Sunday, 7 December 1919 a company called The Coterie of Friends gave an orchestral concert of Coleridge-Taylor works in Wigmore Hall, London. My father, now calling himself Wendell Bruce-James, wrote the analytical notes for the programme, a copy of which Green sent to me.

Jeffrey Green had known a pianist called Amy Barbour James (no relation) who was born of Guyanese parents in 1906 in England. She died in 1988 aged 82. She knew Bruce Wendell and said he was an excellent pianist. Green mentioned one or two of the concerts Bruce had been involved with, details of which were confirmed by Howard Rye.

Between 1919 and 1921 Bruce performed with the Southern Syncopated Orchestra; Rye has written in depth about this group of musicians. The SSO toured Britain and the Continent and famous amongst its personnel were Sydney Bechet (clarinet) and Buddie Gilmore (drums); Bruce, using several variations of his name, played the organ. This information about the Southern Syncopated Orchestra was completely new to me; it had never been mentioned by Mum or any other member of the family.

Then, on Sunday, 7 June Val telephoned to say that she had contacted someone still living in New York who had known my father. It was James Ingram Fox who described Bruce Wendell as 'my past friend'. I telephoned Ingram. My heart pounded as I made the call; this was indeed another exciting moment, yet a daunting one too. Ingram said he had fond memories of my father, and we agreed to meet. Amba refused to come with me to New York; she said that she couldn't bear to sit and listen to Bruce's praises being sung, and I understood her feelings but, having come this far, I had to try to complete the journey.

Nineteen

The sea is not quite as glassy as it was on Thursday, but it is tolerably smooth, & of course I have by this time almost forgotten that I am on a ship. I find myself eating about twice as much as on shore, the air & the comparatively active life on board give one an excellent appetite. The food is excellent in quality, & overwhelming in quantity. Breakfast 7.30–9.30 (I usually have mine about 8.30). Beef tea or cider on deck at 11.30, lunch at 12.30, tea 4–5, dinner at 7. I shall have put on some weight by the time I get to Demerara, I am quite sure.

And so August 1998 found Herb and me in New York once more on our way to visit Ingram, who lived in a large apartment with beautiful views overlooking the Hudson River. We had decided to visit Ingram as soon as possible because of his great age (unknown, but possibly ninety); we didn't want him to cross the great divide before we'd had a chance to talk to him and I believe he'd already had a couple of heart attacks. Ingram had said in an earlier telephone conversation that he would leave the door of his apartment ajar and that we should just admit ourselves. We climbed the stairs of the large block, made our way to his door, which was propped open with a walking stick, knocked and entered. He was sitting in a chair, very elegantly turned out in suit, waistcoat and tie. On a low table nearby were several small bottles of medication. He seemed to be delighted to see me, but appeared to be slightly cautious of Herb (he later told me that he had thought he wouldn't like my husband – I can't imagine why – but was surprised to discover that he did), and he was obviously a great admirer of the ladies. Before our visit I had sent him a photograph of myself and this was propped prominently on a side table. The wall of one room was completely covered with what seemed like hundreds of photographs of women; it was indeed a gallery of glamour. Ingram had a friendly and entertaining personality and made us very welcome, playing one of his two grand pianos for us, and he talked about his 'past friend' with affection. Unfortunately for me, he didn't know, or couldn't remember, what illness had taken Bruce off. Ingram wasn't able to give me much more information about Bruce Wendell than I already had, but he did a lot of reminiscing and gave me two copies of photographs of Bruce; one was a group photo entitled 'Honouring Mr Bruce Wendell' taken from *The Guianan Christmas Annual* (British Guiana) 1938. The caption referred to him as the 1910 Guiana Scholar 'who has become a noted pianist in London' and who 'was entertained at luncheon by a large number of his admirers' (still no mention of a family in England). The other photograph was on a concert programme that Bruce Wendell had given, again at the Town Hall on West 43rd Street, New York, during the 1945–'46 season. This photograph portrays an older, rather wistful looking Bruce. It struck me that Bruce Wendell had clung to his past without really having a present.

When Adam was next in New York he also called on Ingram, who phoned me the following day to say how delighted he'd been to meet Bruce Wendell's grandson, and Adam also enjoyed the occasion, describing it to me in detail when he came home.

I had carried with me a photograph of Marjie, Amba and myself which must have been taken at the time that Bruce left

England, perhaps for him to carry on the tour; Mum would never have been able to afford to pay for a studio photograph later. I showed the photo to Ingram, who gazed at it silently for quite a long time. Then he murmured, almost to himself, 'To think that he had two such beautiful daughters. I want to cry!'

He then added that he knew that Bruce had had (past tense) a white girlfriend or wife, but that he had never mentioned children in all the time the two of them were acquainted. Ingram said, too, that had he known about Bruce leaving us all he would 'have given him hell over it'. So, Ingram and Bruce had been friends for thirty-five years and never once in all that time had Bruce talked about deserting his wife or mentioned his children, something that I find almost gruesome. Although he may not have wanted to admit that he had left his marriage behind in London, it would seem to be characteristic for a father – well, a normal father at least – to mention his children, if not to the general public at least to a close friend who also had children, as Ingram did. Bruce Wendell was not a normal father.

'Another friend, George, knew Bruce,' Ingram told me. 'George's opinion was that Bruce wasn't as good a pianist as he thought he was.' Ingram added that Bruce's concerts were not well reviewed, so it seems that opinions about his talents were conflicting.

Then Ingram went on to say that he thought Bruce would have been better off in England; he didn't manage, in the United States, to perform regularly but he taught piano a little and supplemented his small income by proof-reading English books. That information I found more than a little pitiable. I think I agree, too, that Bruce would have been better off in England; if only he'd just hung on things would probably have worked out, especially with Mum beside him. There would have been some form of employment for him during the war and afterwards the situation would surely have improved, although, of course, that's easy to say in hindsight; one can't help but sympathise with the fact that his lack of progress must have been very frustrating for him.

I had rather hoped that more children had been born to Bruce within his second marriage and that I would have a half-brother or sister, but Ingram told me that there had been none.

Ingram excitedly telephoned a friend, Professor Clifton O Dummett (Orrin), the son of Eglantine Johnson who was Bruce's classmate all those years ago. 'Guess who I have with me,' he quizzed Orrin. 'Bruce Wendell's daughter!' Orrin, too, was surprised to learn than Bruce Wendell had had a family in London – as Val Wilmer was to say at one time, 'Who'd have expected *you* to come out of the woodwork?' Orrin had much to say about Bruce Wendell. Although he was too young to have been a close friend of Bruce, Orrin did remember him returning from Guyana (where he had stayed in the finest hotels, he said) with the Russian singer, Zorina, and he'd been told that when on stage there was nobody like Bruce Wendell. He described Bruce's stage presence as 'class'. He went on to tell me about his mother's school-time association with my father. According to Orrin, when Bruce arrived in the States he became very good friends with a Dr C Fitzgerald Layne and they became such good companions that when Bruce was having a difficult time financially he stayed with the Laynes; it was they who introduced him to Helen Williams, the woman he later married. However, Helen, a social worker, was better off financially; she was the main breadwinner and, being more self-sufficient, wasn't willing to play the subservient role. They later separated and Bruce spent a good amount of time in Dr Layne's home. I gather from this that Bruce never managed to get a home of his own; he and Helen rented two apartments because, according to Ingram, Helen didn't like him to practise the piano in their living space.

Orrin was very sympathetic about my search for my father. He said that he could understand Bruce's desertion only in terms of his being an artist with a particularly unusual background; the fact that he had been an undergraduate at Oxford placed him in a special category and the chances are that he also might have adopted some of the idiosyncrasies of artists – egocentricity and also a certain trace of selfishness and lack of responsibility. This was the view taken by Bob all those years back; he was of the opinion that, based on his personal associations in the Caribbean, many male West Indians were dismissive of their spouses, going their own way when it suited them even when children had been born into the family. Although Orrin believed there was no forgiving him for leaving his family as he had, he thought that Bruce Wendell needed more pity and forgiveness than censureship.

I agree with this to a certain extent, although I can't forgive my father. He is to be pitied, though, because he lost us, his children, and his devoted wife, our mother; also, his hopes of success in the United States were never realised. What I cannot understand is how he thought he could become successful or famous without Mum hearing about it. Had he made up his mind to return to us *when* he had found success? That is what Alfred believes, and maybe he's right. Perhaps it was my father's intention to return only if we could be proud of him, but his reported relationship with Madam Austin and his subsequent marriage to Helen Williams would have altered mightily any such plans. I have no evidence that he ever confided in any of his acquaintances in the United States about his family in England; it may be that he thought they might have disapproved of his marriage to a white woman. Most people would have confessed a guilty secret – I don't mean a life-endangering, criminal secret – to a close friend, if only to assuage their conscience somewhat, perhaps get it off their chest; maybe Bruce never considered any of his acquaintances as close friends. Not to have unburdened himself to anyone over more than thirty years indicates to me either a lack of remorse about his actions or a particularly strong resolve. Either way it looks as though he just didn't care about us. I find that I am no closer to making sense of my father's behaviour than I was at the outset of my search, and I think I must come to the conclusion that he was an egotist and that he used people for his own ends, discarding them when they were no longer required. In 1935 Bruce asked Austin M Noltë in Trinidad to help him give recitals and later to have his concert in New York publicised, yet he didn't even let Noltë know he was leaving for New York and didn't reply to him or thank him when Noltë complied with his request to notify the press. Because of his desertion my mother had to work very, very hard to support the four of us, but had he stayed or returned, my mother would still have had to work hard to support five of us because it does look, sadly, as though my father was not capable of organising his life or of making a living that would adequately sustain a family. I think he may have died a very disappointed man because most of the events of his life seem to have been a failure, on both a personal and professional level. Maybe that sounds harsh, and undoubtedly there were racial problems, but always he seems to have relied on his success at getting a place at Oxford and the acclaim he desired and received seemed to come solely from his compatriots. Orrin says that Bruce frequently had to depend on others for financial support. I am sure that, of our two parents, we were far and away better off with our dear mum, and it's a tragedy that she didn't know it. One characteristic that neither Amba nor I have inherited from our father is disloyalty. Both of Bruce's daughters have been as faithful to their families as our mother was to us and to him.

I know, too, that Bruce owed taxes in Britain; one day, not long after the end of the war, when Mum and I were alone in the flat in Holloway, someone from the Inland Revenue called asking where Bruce Wendell could be found. I remember the occasion well; Mum worried that she would be liable for the debt, the amount of which she didn't know but which she would certainly not have been able to find. The tax authorities had managed to track her down after more than a decade despite the many times she had moved to a different address. Was that debt another (big enough) reason for Bruce to decide not to return to England?

After leaving Ingram, Herb and I went to the address in Madison Avenue where Helen Williams lived. She was not there and on making enquiries of the office managers we were told that it was believed she had been admitted to a nursing home 'many years ago' and had died. I tried to obtain Bruce's and Helen's marriage certificate from Vital Records, but it couldn't be traced despite several efforts on my (and Adam's) behalf. This was a great disappointment because I would have liked to know how Bruce described himself when he remarried; whether as a bachelor, divorcé or widower. But maybe they hadn't, in fact, married. Although Ingram had told me quite firmly that it was most unlikely that Bruce would have left a will, because he had nothing to bequeath, I did carry out a search for one at the Surrogate Courts Probate Division and drew a blank. Whilst basically this was what I expected – I certainly didn't believe that I would have been a beneficiary even had he left any money or possessions – I did have a crazy but forlorn hope that there might have been a message for Amba and me; that would have been something, at least. And I had by now become fairly certain that Helen Williams couldn't have known all about her husband's former life in England.

There are times when I can hardly believe my own story. To think that I had a father who deserted us so cruelly; that I had a father who apparently didn't want to know anything about his two little girls; that I had a father, talented and intelligent and cultured, whom I never knew and who never knew me; that I had a father *who didn't love me or want me.* The factor I find hardest to accept is that we didn't know each other and I wish I'd taken an interest in him and tried to find him before he died. In the 1960s I heard of a woman – a relative of a friend – whose husband disappeared whilst their only child was a baby. The man's clothing was found abandoned on a beach but his body was never discovered and it was assumed that he had committed suicide. About eleven years later the child, a girl, was alone at home one afternoon when someone called to mend the television and the girl let him in and showed him where the set was. Whilst dismantling it, the stranger made conversation with the girl, asking what her interests were and what she liked best about school, and so on. He also asked about the girl's mother. He was friendly and seemed to be kind; the girl was relaxed in his company, enjoying the conversation and answering his questions. He left, and when the mother returned home and the girl explained that she had admitted the TV repair man she was told, to her surprise, that there was nothing wrong with the set and no one had been called to repair it. It was then discovered that the television had been taken apart and that it wasn't working any more; it was therefore supposed that the bogus repairer had, in fact, been the child's father. That story fascinated me; I would find it heart-warming and comforting if I discovered that my father had found a way, anonymously, to find out where we were and how we were getting along. At least that would have shown that he cared a little. There are many others who have been deserted in similar circumstances – we aren't the first and won't be the last – but what I find so unbelievable is that Bruce left Amba and me here in England, in a place where he himself had felt ostracised because of his colour, where he had received an enviable education, where he had married a white woman and had put her into a decidedly unenviable situation, and then had just taken off as free as air, leaving us all in abject poverty whilst he swanned around the world living in the best hotels and being entertained by governors on their yachts.

But his reward was, sadly for him, failure to achieve the success he yearned for.

Twenty

Monday Dec 9th

We have had a radiogram from Larsen that we open in Trinidad on Saturday next the 14th. He wires 'Open Humphreys Theatre 14th Shipterdons publicity. Excellent booking'. So I am sticking to my cabin & my music books rather a lot these days. We reach B'dos on Wednesday at 11 a.m. & Trinidad on Thursday at dawn. That only gives a couple of days on shore before kicking off. This will come back from B'dos, & we shall not see Larsen till reaching T'dad. So I'll write again from there.

He didn't write again from Trinidad, nor ever again.

Just after Bob's death I was invited by Nuffield College, where I was still working part-time, to apply for the vacancy which had come about for an Admissions Secretary and was duly appointed to that post. I hadn't worked full-time for years and, still not completely confident, I wasn't sure whether I would be able to handle the job but decided to pluck up courage and give it a try; I intended to stay in the position just as long as it took me to recover from the bereavement. As it turned out I came to enjoy the work so much that I stayed for another twelve years; it turned out to be the longest job I'd ever had, and then in early 1991 I transferred to Lincoln College as their College Secretary. By that time Graham had settled in Poole in Dorset. He had, on leaving college, been employed by the Oxford Playhouse and gone on tour with the theatre. One of their venues had been Poole and there he had met and fallen for a young woman so decided to stay. Their association didn't last long, but he enjoyed living close to the sea and had made friends. Adam was living in London, later moving to the United States. Both my sons have travelled extensively around the world with their careers.

I enjoyed my work at Lincoln College but after three years, Herb, who had his own business as a freelance book-designer, decided that he needed to become computerised and asked me, as I had been trained to use a computer, to join him as his typesetter. He had, of course, been educated in the traditional ways of book design, but technology had now taken over. I had by then worked for eighteen years at the university so I felt it was time for a change; all Herb's clients had modernised their ways and most, if not all, were using electronic desktop publishing applications, requiring their freelancers to follow suit. Herb was not computer literate at that time so he underwent an intensive course in computing and electronic design. I resigned from the college and Herb and I worked together for another nine years or so; I learned a lot about book design and I found it enjoyable and fulfilling. Now that I was not confined to taking my annual summer holiday during the university vacations we were able to enjoy holidays in the spring or autumn and, in April 1999, we decided on the spur of the moment to visit Antigua.

This was a good idea, I thought, and it was a trip I looked forward to with much excitement. I'm not much of a one for travelling but this was different; this was part of my quest. When we arrived in Antigua we were almost knocked off our feet by the sudden heat of the West Indies as we disembarked from the plane, and we were greeted cordially at the tiny airport. It's the only Caribbean country I've ever been to and whenever I mentioned to any of the local people that my father was born there we received even greater hospitality, as though being welcomed back into the family. St John's is a pretty, interesting town, bustling with friendly and seemingly happy people, and it's possibly one of the only countries I have been to where people are so content that you see no one begging or down and out. It is also so small that we managed to visit all the places we needed to go to. We were able to search the public records and to look at Bruce's original birth certificate, and I also searched for records of any other members of the family. The original, antiquated birth records were quite an eye-opener; a link to the past not just because of their subject matter but also because of the difference in descriptive terminology. At the time of Bruce's birth, apart from the usual entries such as 'Date', 'Sex of child', 'Parents' names', etc., there was a further column headed 'Complexion'. In this column one of the words 'White', 'Coloured' or 'Black' was recorded. Bruce is described as 'Coloured' on his certificate although, from photographs I have of him, I would have thought he should have been described as 'Black', but it may, perhaps, have been a sign of status in those days to be classified Coloured although it certainly isn't now; when I mentioned this classification to the young Antiguan woman who was the hotel guide she asked, with a laugh, whether my father was the colour blue! The copy birth certificate that had been sent to me didn't include this description of complexion, which has now evidently found its way into oblivion. I also tracked down the records of Bruce's Uncle Joseph and of two cousins, but could find no siblings for Bruce. His cousins were both classified Black; they were Thirzie (or Thirzia) Louise James, born 21 March 1894, and Edward Herman Theodore James, born 16 January 1896.

The little register office in St John's was amazingly untidy and disordered. There was a small waiting room, perhaps about fifteen feet square, with shabby furniture, one or two chairs for visitors and heaps of bound volumes of original certificates that appeared to be in no particular sequence, some of them broken at the spines. Two or three clerks were dealing with visitors, most of whom seemed to be young mothers registering the births of their babies. I was handed the volume I requested and then had to use a pile of cardboard boxes to rest it on as there was no appropriate table top or shelf. When I got to the document I was looking for I found that Bruce Wendell's certificate had been defaced with written comments made, very possibly, at the time I requested the copy, and other pages in the volume were about to become entirely loose. We did, though, visit another modern building where archives were stored and that was completely different; the documents were carefully protected and preserved, as those of us in a more modern world have come to expect. I am making no criticism here; merely a statement.

One day we went into a church in St John's but discovered that preparations were being made for a funeral, so we took ourselves outside where there was a view of the town. An elderly gentleman greeted us and asked where we were from and I started to tell him about my family search, mentioning Bruce's uncle who had been an Inspector of Schools. The gentleman seemed to know to whom we referred, and said, 'Oh, that was a long time ago,' and he pointed across the road, adding, 'that was where he lived, although the house he had has since been replaced by another.' Antigua was lovely and its people courteous and friendly, and as I had when I first moved to Oxford, I imagined my father's footsteps on the same streets. Although I learned little more about my father and his family, the trip was quite delightful.

At the beginning of this narrative I mentioned that I felt deprived because I had no opportunity, on leaving school, to embark on higher education; let me now return to that. In the spring of 2002 Herb decided to retire and, as his typesetter, I became redundant. I had tried for many years to write the story of how my family had been deserted but had become overwhelmed with the quantity of information and documentation that had come my way; I needed guidance. I had never been taught how to carry out research or how to get my writing into a readable format. I discovered that Ruskin College, Oxford, ran a Certificate of Higher Education course in Creative Writing and I applied for admission, never dreaming that I would be accepted; I was invited for interview and told that I could expect a decision within two weeks and Alistair Wisker, the Creative Writing tutor who interviewed me, added, 'A *positive* decision.' The letter I later received informing me that I had been offered a place immediately gave me stage-fright again. Could I manage this? Would I dare to take up the offer? Would I make a fool of myself? At sixty-eight I must have been one of the oldest applicants that year. Again I plucked up courage and accepted the place. Here was the opportunity to learn how to put into words my voyage of discovery, and I thought maybe it might work; if you are reading this memoir in a published book, then I have been successful. The course itself turned out to be an astounding adventure and an enlightening experience; the other students in the college were interesting, friendly, knowledgeable, and all were eager to study. Our backgrounds were diverse; we were of all shapes, sizes, colours and ages, but one thing we all had in common: for various reasons none of us had received a higher education and so we were all keen and willing to learn. Some of my fellow-students will always remain my friends; I enjoyed the classes and found the interaction with the others invaluable. One of the bonuses was that Ruskin students get Oxford University Reader's Tickets so that they can use the Bodleian Library and its dependant libraries; as soon as I had been admitted as a Reader and had sworn not to burn the place down, I went into the Radcliffe

Camera, the inside of which I'd wanted to see since arriving in Oxford. (I later learned that employees of the university could be admitted as Readers if they have a good enough reason but, whilst employed by the university, I had been unaware of this.) The Bodleian provided me with some of the bibliographical information that I needed; I revelled in being an 'Oxford' student! I did well on the course and was encouraged by my tutors to apply for a place at university. By now I wasn't quite so timid about my limitations and I was subsequently offered an unconditional place on their Media and Creative Writing BA course by Middlesex University, entering in the second year because the Cert HE which I had earned at Ruskin took the place of the first year of a BA course. Here was a triumph over my father's desertion; Betty, Bob's sister, sent me a card bearing a button-badge that said 'I did it! And I did it good!' which I wore (under my collar) for weeks. Herb was proud of me and so was the rest of the family, and I was very pleased with myself. Although I would be seventy-one at the end of the course I would, if successful, have achieved a mighty victory. Unfortunately, though, I decided to withdraw from the course shortly after the beginning of the first semester; as a non-residential student I found the journey to and from north London too taxing; it was impracticable and stressful. Although this was a disappointing decision to have to make, it was at least of my own choosing and I still had the satisfaction of knowing that I had been considered university material.

But what decision have I come to about my father? What sense have I made of his deserting us? Heaven only knows; I am little the wiser. He married my mother and had two children; she told me that she was pursued by him for six months so he must have fallen in love with her. The big mistake the two of them made, I think, was producing two daughters; a family was too much of a responsibility for Bruce's artistic temperament and it is highly likely that both Amba and I were unplanned. Bruce should never have married; had my parents met today they would just have lived together for a while, but in those days only the aristocracy, it seems, could get away with extra-marital affairs with impunity. To have lived openly in what was then termed 'sin' would not have been an option for Mary. Alfred may be right when he says that Bruce embarked on the tour in order to improve his situation and make a better life for his family, but when he met Madam Austin in Trinidad he decided then to start a new life. Whatever sort of relationship that was I shall never know, but clearly it didn't last. Yet that encounter may have been the main reason he never came back to us; if, as a religious man, he had had some sort of adulterous relationship he may have felt he couldn't return to his wife. He was unsuccessful in getting recognition as a concert pianist, that is now clear. Perhaps he wasn't a good enough musician; maybe he was unlucky; possibly he felt that he couldn't return to Mary because he couldn't face up to failure. And what about his marriage to Helen (if it existed) which, apart from not enduring, would have been, it seems, a bigamous one? Did he never worry that he would be discovered? I would speculate that Bruce Wendell's life was unhappy and unfulfilled. He had stated that his life, unless lived in music, was not worth living and I find it in my heart to feel sorrow for him.

I had originally decided to entitle this memoir '*Unforgettable*' because I find it impossible to believe that Bruce really forgot Mum; he must have found it necessary to force himself to put her and us out of his mind.

I later traced Bruce's obituary in *The New York Times* of Friday, August 16 1968 (page 33). Here it is:

*WENDELL—Bruce, Concert Pianist. Departed this life
on Aug. 13, 1968, after a long illness. Survived by wife,
Helen and cousin, Herman James. Funeral Services
private.*

Survived by cousin Herman James? That, I find pathetic. My
father had so few relatives he could acknowledge, that only
his cousin could be pulled into the grieving scenario beside the
second and, possibly, illicit wife. (I tried once more but was
still unable to trace a marriage certificate for Bruce and
Helen.) Perhaps his cousin had stayed in contact with Bruce
and remained close to him; I knew from Val Wilmer that
Herman James had gone to the United States but that his sister,
Thirzia Louise, had remained in Antigua. Of course, whoever
posted the obituary could not have known that Bruce had, in
fact, been survived by his lawful wife, Mary, by his two
daughters, Amba and Ann, and by his four grandchildren,
Neil, Wendy, Graham and Adam, not to mention a
stepdaughter, Margery, and her children, Clifford, Hilary and
Jeffrey; maybe he had, in fact, forgotten all about us by the
time of his long illness. And so he got away with his treachery;
no one appeared to know that he had a legitimate family in
England. If only... if only I had found him before he died so
that he had to confront his disloyalty, had to face up to it and
to us. Yet on the other hand I'm glad that Mum didn't know
the full extent of his faithlessness.

However, based on Bruce's obituary I looked up Edward
Herman James on the genealogical site of The Church of
Jesus Christ of Latter Day Saints and discovered that an
Edward James, born on the same day as our Herman, died in
February 1969, less than a year after Bruce passed away.
Hoping there might have been descendants, I searched for
Herman's obituary but drew a complete blank. Maybe he had

never married. My search for any distant relatives had come to a full stop.

I have conflicting emotions about my father. I have surely conveyed to the reader that I am bitter and resentful over his uncaring treatment of us and it was, without doubt, uncaring, so I think I have every reason to feel as I do. I hate what he did to us but on the other hand, though, I have found some of the revelations of great interest and, strangely, I feel proud that, although not a graduate, he was at least an undergraduate at one of the foremost universities in the world and that I am the product of a cultured man. However, that pride is stolen from me by the fact that I didn't have the chance to know him, to talk to him, to be his daughter, and these factors leave a huge void inside; a hollow feeling in my heart. It is absolutely apparent that he had no concern for his daughters, otherwise why didn't he at least contact us or take an interest in our futures? He might not have felt able to return to us but he could have explained and we could have got to know one another. He owed us that at least.

Has Bruce Wendell left any sort of legacy behind him in England? Not much. Firstly, he considered entering the Church ministry so he must have had strong religious beliefs; secondly, he studied Jurisprudence at Oxford; thirdly, he was a musician. Amba's younger child, Wendy, is a devoted, church-going Christian; her son, Neil, is a successful lawyer in England; my older son, Graham, is a qualified theatre sound and lighting technician who also composes electronic music; and my younger son, Adam, is a musician who has had a certain amount of success and a huge following both with his former band, *Swervedriver*, and also as a solo guitarist and singer/songwriter. So maybe there is some small legacy from Bruce to his grandchildren.

Amba's skin colour is lighter than my own and her two children and five grandchildren have inherited absolutely no physical similarity to Bruce; they are all white-skinned and it is impossible to see any trace of African blood in any of them. Graham's skin colour is lighter than mine, and Adam's is lighter still. So far I have no grandchildren and if that situation remains Bruce Wendell's physical legacy will die out completely in England. It might all have been so different. I'm glad I searched for and found him; I'm sad that he gave my mother so much unhappiness and, because of her circumstances, caused Marjie, Amba and me to have had such a miserable few wartime years; I'm sorry I didn't know him; and I'm sorrier still that he didn't know Amba and me and his four grandchildren. Also it frustrates me, somewhat, that he didn't see what a splendid job our mother did in overcoming the problems he bequeathed to her despite all the obstacles; she even left a small sum of money on her death. I salute my mother; her memory is dear to Marjie, Amba and me, and to our children. There was an occasion when we were all together at her home, and she looked around at us all, at her daughters and their husbands and children, and gave a smile of satisfaction. Then aloud, she said – and I believe she was saying it to herself and not to the assembled family – she said, 'My girls are all right now.'

In our hearts our mother, Mary, will for ever be unforgettable.

Twenty-one

*'...I the LORD your God am a jealous God, visiting the
iniquity of the fathers upon the children to the third and
fourth generation...' (Deuteronomy 5: 9.)*

In August 2003, at just about the time I was trying to complete
this record, Amba's husband, Alf, died after a long and painful
illness; he had suffered for many years from diabetes and renal
failure. They had been married forty-eight years and all
members of the family had been devoted to each other, as had
Marjie's family and mine. Not one of us, Marjie, Amba nor I,
has celebrated a golden wedding, and along with the three of
us, our children and grandchildren have grieved deeply
throughout terrible illness and death.

During my childhood, and especially whilst we were living
with the Salvationists, the above Biblical text niggled at me
and over the years I have thought about it a lot. Were Amba
and I and our descendants going to be punished, by a harsh
and cruel God, just because our father had acted sinfully? I
have made it plain that now I don't believe in the existence of
a God or that the Holy Bible is the word of a God even though
I appreciate that many of its tenets are commendable, but what
I do believe is that a God who would visit the iniquity of the
fathers upon children who were innocent of sin would appear
to be a merciless and unforgiving being (I know that,
according to the Bible, even children are not innocent of sin
but you will understand my point). I asked questions about the

text and the answer I would urge others, whether God-fearing, agnostic or atheist, to take note of is the one I received from The Internet Bible College* who interpreted it as being a case of 'like father, like son'. The son would copy the sinful father, and the grandson would become even more loose living which would also affect his children. In our case, I'm glad to say, Bruce Wendell's behaviour has not unfavourably influenced his two daughters in any way; on the contrary, his children have inherited their mother's sense of duty and loyalty. Nevertheless, I think that Bruce Wendell did have a Christian belief and he, it would seem, didn't care what became of his children or about the sins of the fathers.

---

* www.geocities.com/Athens/Delphi/4027/

Koninklÿke Nederlandsche Stoomboot
Maatschappÿ, Amsterdam

M.S. "Colombia"

Sunday Evening Dec 1st
My dear Mary
Today has been a quiet one for me. Last night
I turned in soon after dinner, about 9.40 I
suppose, & before long I was fast asleep; but
before falling off I could feel them weigh
anchor & get going. The voyage is on the
rough side so far, & this morning I decided
that the horizontal position was best; so I
stayed in bed, & had some breakfast brought
me there. At about 2.30 I had a bath (salt-
water), followed by a brisk shower (fresh-
water), & returned to bed. At first the Steward
came and cleared up a bit; & then I shaved,
got my clavier into position, did some other
sorting-up, & got dressed. It is now 6.45 & I
am writing this before going into dinner,
which is at 7. Last night I enjoyed a fine
dinner. Tonight it will, I suppose, be just as
fine – but the question is whether I shall be
able to enjoy it! I expect the number of diners
tonight will be far less than yesterday; the
purser says that by about Tuesday we should
strike the calmer part of the voyage.

I will try to write some short account of the journey day by day; so by the time this reaches you it will be quite a serial letter.

Monday evening Dec 2nd
Last night was a blower, & no doubt about it. After an excellent dinner, followed by coffee in the social room - where the orchestra played (violin, cello, & piano) - I went off early to bed. I soon got off to sleep, having locked myself into my cabin, but before dozing off was conscious that the ship was rolling a bit; however during the night I woke up to find that we were in the midst of a gale all right, & I could hear from the snippets of conversation that some neighbour of mine had to turn out, owing to his port-holes being stove in by an enormous wave. Luckily for him the pieces of glass did not actually hit him. All this I learned later today, as I refused to budge at the time & finally went off to sleep again. Today I decided to appear for lunch, & found myself thoroughly enjoying a huge meal. After that I retired to rest again, reading in my cabin until 6.15 when I bathed and dressed & now I shall be going into dinner.

Tuesday afternoon 3.45 p.m.
Today I am writing rather earlier. I was up for breakfast at 8 o'clock this morning, &

enjoyed the meal thoroughly. Sat & read on
deck after that until lunch-time, when I felt
that to have lunch would about make me
bust. Why I finished breakfast I suppose round
about 9, & at 11.15 the deck-steward handed
out beef-tea & a biscuit, then fancy asking
one to lunch at 12.30. And what a breakfast!
Grape Fruit, Omelette with Bacon, Brown
Bread & Butter galore, 2 Buns with Butter ad
lib., Marmalade, Coffee.

. . . .

So instead of going in to lunch I had an
orange & a pear on deck. I then went over to
the Second Class to see Dr James, & spent an
hour chatting with him. He is the same as
ever, inclined a bit to brood on unpleasant,
rather than enjoy & make the most of, the
pleasant occurrences in life. So back to some
more reading. From 4 o'clock till 5 tea is
available, & after a cup I shall retire, until
my bath at 6.15.

Last night I played a bit. The piano in the
Music Room is a Grotrian-Steinweg Grand,
rather the worse for sea-air & wear, but quite
playable. Zorina would not be satisfied until
she asked the purser to let me play a while
instead of the band, so I played the Beethoven
Rondo in G & the Scherzo from the Chopin
Sonata. The Captain & Officers & their parties
applauded very much, & off I went to bed,
satisfied that the fingers were in working

order. They wanted Z to sing but she would not.

The other passengers are gradually thawing. Z was placed at the ship's doctor's table, there being only one vacant place there. I told the Chief Steward that I did not wish to sit with any strangers who might not want me with them; so I sit in great state on my own. There are others, I notice, who like their own company. But is is rather amusing how people, & some of the nicest passengers, gradually are going out of their way to talk to me.

There is quite a large number of wealthy folk, evidently, who go out to the West Indies, especially Barbados, year by year, in quest of health. We have advertised our tour with the Captain, & the word has gone round the ship; so we are doing a bit of advertising, by the way.

Well, darling, I do hope you are settling down gradually to the little while of separation which is but the prelude, I hope with all my heart & soul, to my return to a much better position for you & all my other loved ones. I know that I have so much about me to distract & occupy my thoughts, that it is perhaps easier for me than for you; but, believe me, dearest, I miss you, & shall continue, I know, to miss you during these months. But they will soon pass, & we shall be together again, you & Amba & Anne & Marjery & me. So chins up, old girl.

Now, I'm going to tea & a rest afterwards.

Wednesday 1.30
Well dear, here is the next instalment of the journal, continued from just before tea yesterday.

I did not take tea after all, but disappeared into my cabin for a rest instead, not turning out again until the bath steward called me at 6 o'clock. Bath, then dinner. By this time the weather had definitely quieted down, & kept smooth during the night, until today one wonders at times whether we are even moving. But moving we are all right, for we have covered the following distances so far—

	miles
Saturday night to noon Sunday	151
Noon Sunday to noon Monday	297
Monday-Tuesday	340
Tuesday-Today	384
	872 [sic]
	miles in all

The weather is definitely milder today, & the deck sports enthusiasts are getting ready. So far I am sticking to library books, which I find interesting & good company. I would like to find a fellow chess-fiend, but no luck so far. Night before last Zorina told me she played chess; but when we sat down to it in the smoke room, it turned out that she meant 'draughts', at which she beat me two games, the first easily, & the second through my mistakes, as I have not played draughts for ages.

Last night I played the piano a bit again, to the apparent interest & enjoyment of various people. After that I took a turn on the deck, & retired early. I have decided to get in as much rest as possible while I can, for I look forward with some apprehension to all the social events people may try to drag me into when I get over the other side.

It is marvellous how the improved weather has fetched ailing passengers out today. The ship is alive with conversation & one sees faces that had not appeared at all before. The doctor told me this morning that his list has now gone down from 75 to 19!

What a difference in one day! The sea as I look out from the writing room, is almost motionless, & those huge white-toothed rollers that kept us company till yesterday are almost forgotten. Some time this evening we shall pass by the Canary Islands & then we strike straight across, I understand, for the West Indies.

I wonder how you & the children are going on. Zorina has been giving marvellous accounts of you & them to people. We are of the highest aristocracy & position in England! I had not realised that so many people were attracted to the W.I. at this time of the year, but we have on board, Lt General This, & Sir George that, & Major What's-It, & so on & so forth. Lord Help Us is not in the list, though.

Well, darling, that's all for now. More next

time. My thoughts are with you, and my
fondest prayers & hopes with you all. My
tenderest love, as always, for you, sweet one.
Au revoir!

Saturday 12 noon.
I am afraid I have missed two days, dear, but
somehow I have not felt in the mood to settle
down to write. There has been little news,
except that we are getting every moment into
more delightfully tropical weather. I have
been working a lot on the Clavier, & yesterday
did an hour's rehearsal with Zorina.

I have found some chess opponents now &
had a game or two. People are altogether
thawing more & more, & I think the concerts
will get plenty of publicity through our fellow
passengers.

The sea is not quite as glassy as it was on
Thursday, but it is tolerably smooth, & of
course I have by this time almost forgotten
that I am on a ship. I find myself eating
about twice as much as on shore, the air & the
comparatively active life on board give one
an excellent appetite. The food is excellent in
quality, & overwhelming in quantity.
Breakfast 7.30-9.30 (I usually have mine
about 8.30). Beef tea or cider on deck at
11.30, lunch at 12.30, tea 4-5, dinner at 7. I
shall have put on some weight by the time I
get to Demerara, I am quite sure.

My one regret, my dear one, is that you are not here to share all this with me; but be patient a little longer, & we will triumph yet. My thoughts are with you often in the day, always when I lay myself down in my bunk. The time will soon pass by & when I come back you will, Heaven helping us, be proud of your Daddy.

I hope Amba & Margery are being good girls & that you are keeping cheerful & looking forward, forgetting the difficulties of the moment. There are some things I want you to do. First, will you collect my post once a week or so from Aggrey House, & send it on to me for the present c/o ~~Queen's College~~ General Post Office,

Georgetown
Demerara

Also there is a dress waistcoat in the top drawer (black); please send it to same address. I collected the jacket & a pair of trousers. The suit will be a standby to save the new one. Thank you dear.

Monday Dec 9th
We have had a radiogram from Larsen that we open in Trinidad on Saturday next the 14th. He wires 'Open Humphreys Theatre 14th Shipterdons publicity. Excellent booking'. So I am sticking to my cabin & my music books rather a lot these days. We reach B'dos on Wednesday at 11 am & Trinidad on Thursday

at dawn. That only gives a couple of days on shore before kicking off. This will come back from B'dos, & we shall not see Larsen till reaching T'dad. So I'll write again from there.

Now I'll close dear, in case I don't get a chance to write again before Trinidad.

Well, darling, all my tenderest love to you & the bairns & my thoughts always.

With fondest kisses, Mary darling, from your Daddy.

Bibliography

Algernon Aspinall, *The British West Indies*, London, 1912, p 296

Barbados Advocate, Monday, December 2 1935, p 10

Bruce-James, Wendell, 'The Ideal Kinema Organ' in the *Melody Maker (Music in the Kinema)*, pp 1034–1035

Craig, E S and Gibson, W M, eds., *Oxford University Roll of Service*, (Oxford, 1920), p 557

The Daily Argosy, Friday, December 6 1935, p 5

——7 January 1936

Dunbar, Rudolph, *Daily Chronicle*, Georgetown, December 22 1935, p 16

Green, Jeffrey P, *Edmund Thornton Jenkins: The life and times of an American black composer 1894–1926*, Greenwood Press, Westport, Conn., London, 1982, pp 66, 80–81, 85, 152

The Guianan Christmas Annual (British Guiana), 1938

The Jamaica Times, Saturday, September 19 1936, p 34

Oxford University Gazette, June 4 1913, p 932

Rye, Howard, 'Visiting Firemen 15' in *Storyville*, 1990, pp 173 and 176

The Times, Wed., January 1 1930, p 6

Trinidad Express, 10 February 1975, p 16

Wendell, Bruce, *Daily Chronicle*, Georgetown, 7 January 1936, p 6

Printed in the United Kingdom
by Lightning Source UK Ltd.
116993UKS00001B/12